# OUR RESULTS-DRIVEN TESTING CULTURE

## How It Adversely Affects Students' Personal Experience

*Lyn Lesch*

**Rowman & Littlefield Education**
Lanham, Maryland • Toronto • Plymouth, UK
2007

Published in the United States of America
by Rowman & Littlefield Education
A Division of Rowman & Littlefield Publishers, Inc.
A wholly owned subsidiary of The Rowman & Littlefield Publishing Group, Inc.
4501 Forbes Boulevard, Suite 200, Lanham, Maryland 20706
www.rowmaneducation.com

Estover Road
Plymouth PL6 7PY
United Kingdom

Copyright © 2007 by Lyn Lesch

*All rights reserved.* No part of this publication may be reproduced, stored in a retrieval system, or transmitted in any form or by any means, electronic, mechanical, photocopying, recording, or otherwise, without the prior permission of the publisher.

British Library Cataloguing in Publication Information Available

**Library of Congress Cataloging-in-Publication Data**

Lesch, Lyn, 1948–
  Our results-driven testing culture : how it adversely affects students' personal experience / Lyn Lesch.
    p. cm.
  ISBN-13: 978-1-57886-661-8 (hardback : alk. paper)
  ISBN-10: 1-57886-661-8 (hardback : alk. paper)
  ISBN-13: 978-1-57886-662-5 (pbk. : alk. paper)
  ISBN-10: 1-57886-662-6 (pbk. : alk. paper)
  1. Educational tests and measurements—Social aspects. 2. Educational psychology. I. Title.
  LB3051.L4542 2007
  371.8019—dc22
                                                    2007018147

∞™ The paper used in this publication meets the minimum requirements of American National Standard for Information Sciences—Permanence of Paper for Printed Library Materials, ANSI/NISO Z39.48-1992.
Manufactured in the United States of America.

# CONTENTS

INTRODUCTION v

1  OUR RESULTS-DRIVEN
   TESTING CULTURE 1

2  LEARNING AND EXPERIENCE 9

3  EVALUATIONS AND
   DISEMBODIED LEARNING 23

4  COGNITIVE LEARNING
   AND STUDENT IMPRESSIONS 43

5  ADULT PRECONCEPTIONS
   AND STUDENT NEEDS 55

6  DEVELOPMENTAL CONCERNS 71

7  A JUST EQUILIBRIUM 85

## CONTENTS

| | | |
|---|---|---|
| 8 | THE STUDENT'S OWN EXPERIENCE | 101 |
| 9 | DIAGNOSIS AND EVALUATION | 117 |
| 10 | CONTINUUMS OF LEARNING | 129 |

**ABOUT THE AUTHOR** 141

# INTRODUCTION

From 1991 to 2003, I was the founder and director of The Children's School, a small private school in Evanston, Illinois, for students between the ages of six and fourteen. Enrollment reached as high as thirty students, but most years it was closer to twenty. The mission of the school was to provide an environment for students in which they could actually maintain control of their existence after they had walked inside the schoolhouse door, rather than be immediately subjected to adult preconceptions concerning how children should be educated or to the overly rigid daily scheduling or predetermined curricula that one often finds in other schools.

In other words, I was interested in finding out what sort of educational environment might evolve if I gave the students the greatest possible voice in how they would approach both their learning and the school environment itself, and in which they could also engage in meaningful learning on a regular basis.

Prior to founding my school, I had taught in more traditional schools and had come to see many of the preexisting methodologies and philosophies employed there as actual barriers standing between the students in the school and the healthy evolution of their individual experiences. Therefore, originally I was primarily interested in attempting to provide a learning environment in which students would not be subjected to many of the controlling aspects of more traditional schools. Specifically, I wanted to eliminate much of the unnatural adult authority that predetermines both their curricula and the structure of their actual school days in order to achieve certain adult-conceived external validations of their learning, such as good grades and higher test scores.

However, as the school evolved, and as more and more students became enrolled in it, I came to realize that there is so much more to providing a healthy learning environment than merely removing many of the controls that one finds in more results-driven, traditional schools.

If significant learning is to take place in young people's lives, they certainly need the correct amount of guidance and direction. Otherwise, they will not acquire the necessary information, knowledge, and skills that they need in order to function to their potential in the world they will be entering. At the same time, by not giving young people the necessary amount of direction and guidance, the message will be imparted to them that they are less capable than they might actually be, and consequently that is just what they will become.

Yet, as my school grew and even flourished, I learned how imperative it is that this guidance and direction must evolve primarily from careful observation of each student's experience in the school. Otherwise, if one is adopting any sort of preconceived philosophy aimed in advance at achieving certain results, even if it is being implemented with the best of intentions, then it does not originate with the individual experiences of the students in the school.

# INTRODUCTION

In addition, over time I found that my own progressive thinking concerning the correct education for students in their formative years met the needs of some of the children in the school but did not meet the needs of other children. In fact, I discovered that because the particular progressive philosophy I was espousing tended to attract a number of parents who gave their children more room and less direction than they probably should have had, I was often in the position of having to provide those very limits and direction myself, even though that was not why I had opened the school in the first place.

As a result, I learned a powerful lesson concerning how the actual reasons certain parents are attracted to the philosophy that a particular school employs have a significant effect on the approach that those who teach at the school will have to adopt in order to meet the needs of the students who are being educated there.

So, as time went on, I found that there was something much more important than my own particular values concerning progressive education, values that were formed during my years teaching in other schools. This more important entity was the need to develop an approach toward each student that originated entirely with the experiences and needs of the young person as an individual.

That is, because some students who were enrolled in my school had already developed qualities such as initiative and self-direction, they simply needed to be put in touch with different subject matters of which they might not have been aware or different ways of approaching various areas of learning, and they were off to the races, so to speak. Other students, however, needed quite a bit of guidance and direction in order to learn.

Therefore, a philosophy that had once been based on certain progressive ideas concerning the provision of the proper amount of latitude for students as they learn became one in which it was

## INTRODUCTION

increasingly clear to me that the only truly intelligent approach to educating young people in their formative years is one in which the philosophy grows only from the experiences and needs of each individual student.

Otherwise, there is no way to be sure that the particular approach that a school employs is meeting the needs of its individual students. Yet, at the same time, I knew that the question had to be asked: How does healthy experience evolve in young people as they learn? How does the attempt by each student to make increasing contact with his or her immediate environment as he or she learns from it evolve in a healthy manner?

As this particular question grew uppermost in my mind, I also realized that I was moving ever closer to administering a school for young people in their formative years that had no generalized philosophy or approach. If the approach I employed with each student grew directly from my understanding of what healthy experience and learning were for that particular young person, then I was now simultaneously employing any number of different approaches or methodologies. As a matter of fact, these different approaches eventually ranged all the way from completely self-directed learning for some students to very structured learning with very specific consequences for others.

As this diversity of approaches increasingly became the modus operandi of the school, then the real question over time became, what are the different issues that one needs to consider in providing an environment for young people that attempts to facilitate their personal experiences and their learning in the healthiest manner possible? Consequently, this work is an attempt to examine many of those issues and also to examine them in relation to the results-driven educational landscape that now permeates our culture.

If one does not begin with issues that are fundamental to how learning and personal experience might be bound together in

## INTRODUCTION

young people as a singular, healthy process, then it becomes much more difficult to set up the holistic learning environment that I had in mind during my years with The Children's School. In fact, if one is attempting to set up an educational environment for students in their formative years that is largely based on the evolution of their healthy experience, rather than adopting any sort of preconceived philosophy or methodology aimed primarily at achieving certain empirical results, then ultimately what provides one with the greatest amount of clarity is the question of how young people might make increasingly healthy contact with their immediate environment.

The point is, if we as educators are ever going to develop approaches to educating young people that simultaneously stimulate meaningful learning and foster healthy personal growth, it is important that we take a much closer look at how students might make contact with their world in a much healthier, less neurotic fashion as they learn. We need to do so by carefully considering this aspect of education in relation to the high-stakes, standardized testing culture that now permeates our schools. Whether one agrees with this results-driven trend or not, it has increasingly become the bottom-line reality in contemporary education.

So this, then, is the subject of my work. It concerns the personal experience, developmental issues, and academic learning of students between the ages of six and fourteen. My research laboratory, if one would call it that, has been the twelve years I spent founding, directing, and teaching at The Children's School. In fact, particularly because I allowed the philosophy of the school to evolve out of what I learned during the course of my day-to-day experience with the students there—as difficult and subject to my own errors of judgment as that was at times—rather than operate according to any sort of preconceived philosophy or approach, I was in a truly unique position to observe how healthy, experiential growth might take place in young people as they learn.

## INTRODUCTION

Compared to many other schools that, to various degrees, observe learning and personal interactions of students through the preconceived lens of whatever philosophy or methodology they are employing, I was observing that learning and those interactions only with an eye toward trying to discover exactly what sort of learning environment might allow young people to remain fully grounded in their own experiences. In other words, my view of the environment I was creating was open ended to the extent that I literally didn't know where it would eventually evolve.

And so, because ultimately all I really had in this endeavor were my own efforts to observe the experience of the individual students in the school as clearly as possible, I was able to look at childhood learning and experience with the pristine eyes that are often denied other educators by their own predetermined structures, philosophies, and methodologies.

Also, and of equal importance, because we gave no grades and administered an occasional standardized test only at the request of a student or parent, we were in a unique position to observe how learning evolves in young people if one takes away certain external motivational devices, such as good grades or high test scores.

Out of this clear, unclouded perception, I have come to the conclusion that if we are to improve learning environments for students in their formative years, then we must begin by observing the dynamics of their personal experience much more closely than our results-driven culture presently allows us to do. More specifically, we need to look closely at how young people can both feel in control of their own experience and also consistently complete those experiences as they learn. The ways in which students in their formative years make contact with the world they inhabit—although extremely varied, complex, and personal—also demonstrate possession of their own unique, deep truths.

INTRODUCTION

However, in order to carefully observe these truths, we have to begin by looking at academic learning and personal experience with a completely fresh set of eyes aimed at discovering how these two things might be fused together as a singular process rather than continuing to ignore the latter in favor of achieving certain empirical results. As part of this process, contemporary educators must renew their interest in becoming students of the dynamics of personal experience, much in the same manner as any good scientist attempts to uncover the truths that the physical, organic, or social worlds occasionally yield.

Ultimately, particularly in regard to students in their formative years, academic learning that does not emanate from the personal experience of the learner becomes inevitably a disembodied process in which the inevitable split between mental processes and emotive, developmental issues begins to occur on a regular basis. The results are not only developing psyches that become dulled but also developing human beings who, at an early age, begin to mistrust what their own experiences have to teach, simply because what they learn at school tends to begin and then proceed entirely outside of such experiences.

If we are to reverse this process, we as educators must begin with the actual personal experience and needs of the individual students we are educating and then work outward from there toward creating intelligent approaches and curricula. Conversely, we should not keep clinging to preconceptions and structures that we hope will produce certain external results and to which we expect our students to adapt by limiting and shaping their personal experience. This is indeed the bottom line, the heretofore unanswered question regarding our schools and methods of education: How do we create learning environments for young people in which their learning and their personal experiences are part of a singular, holistic, healthy process?

# OUR RESULTS-DRIVEN TESTING CULTURE

We live in a time in which the standardized test scores that are part of the current national testing program are increasingly becoming the primary indicators of how well students are learning. The so-called success or failure of schools is so tied to these scores that the two have, in fact, often become synonymous.

This is particularly true when things like teacher accountability and school funding are so inextricably tied to test results that there is a genuine fear generated in both teachers and administrators that the scores of their students will not measure up. As a result of this fear, entire curriculums and educational approaches are now being developed with the goal in mind of attempting to be certain that the knowledge, information, and skills that students are assimilating will lead toward the highest possible scores.

Coincidentally, paralleling this trend is the increasingly competitive nature of education itself, a competition that is based largely on empirical results. From test scores of very young children that will give them admittance to the best primary schools to the desire by high school students to receive the grades and

# CHAPTER 1

test scores that will give them admittance to the best colleges, which are increasingly becoming brand names for success, both parents and students seem to be more concerned than ever with external validations of learning.

In addition, there have been many books written concerning the effects, be they positive or negative, that the current national testing program is having on the actual ability of students to learn or on what parents or teachers can do to best prepare those students for success on these tests. Naturally, this is to be expected. Teachers and parents naturally want to know whether the current trend toward the use of empirical results as a primary indication of learning will in fact make students better learners, and they want to know what they can do to facilitate the best possible results in their students or their own children.

However, there seems to be one significant issue concerning the entire results-driven culture in which we now live that has not been adequately addressed: the effect that educational approaches primarily concerned with children achieving the best possible external validations of their learning might have on the evolution of their personal experience. In what ways is the manner in which young people make increasing contact with their world affected by the adult need to structure classroom environments in a manner that produces optimal empirical indications of their learning?

If the primary goal of educating students in their formative years has become one of engendering the best possible external validations of learning, those that can be empirically tested by grades or test scores, then it also becomes inevitable that learning environments will be, more than ever, structured well in advance of students entering them.

This is done, of course, in an attempt to be certain that the environments that students enter will engender learning of subject matter and skills that are part of predetermined curricula that will eventually be evaluated. Then, as this occurs, it also becomes more certain than ever that young people will be increasingly educated according to preconceived approaches based primarily on adult needs to be certain that the best possible results will be generated, and not so much according to the experiences of individual students in different classrooms.

In other words, the cart is put squarely in front of the horse when educators set up environments that they hope will shape the experiences and learning of the individual students in order to produce certain outcomes, rather than actually attempting to create educational milieus out of the truths that such experiences have to offer.

If such were not the case, if schools and classrooms had evolved from the verities of what the experiences of the individual students in them proved to be rather than from our increasingly obsessive need to produce predetermined results, then we would develop much healthier conditions for learning. When educational environments for young people are set up in advance of how the personal experiences of the students in them naturally evolve, then one is already setting up conditions by which those students may well come to feel mistrustful of, and alienated from, their own experiences. This happens simply because there is always the distinct possibility that those aspects of the students' environment that shape their learning will pull them in one direction at the same time that their own interests, curiosities, and tendencies pull them in another.

Fragmentation and mistrust of one's experience go hand in hand. Whenever young people come to feel that what they are experiencing is important to them, and at the same time, that experience is not given proper credence by those who are educating them, then those students are given a powerful negative message about the validity of their own experiences.

Any time students must leave for good an area of study that truly interests them and adhere to a set curriculum that they had

CHAPTER 1

no hand in creating, they are given such a message. Any time students with certain needs come into contact with particular learning environments that don't address those needs because they are created from adult preconceptions concerning what environment will produce the best possible empirical results, those students are given such a message.

Any time young people are not permitted to stay long enough with any strongly experienced impressions because of an approach to learning that has become overly cognitive in nature due to a particular school's need to prepare students for certain external evaluations, they are given such a message. And any time youths come to feel that more personal, developmental issues of theirs are not being met because there is no time for this within their results-driven learning environment, they are given such a message.

These are some of the ways in which young people today become mistrustful of what their experiences tell them because of how they are being educated in our schools. And once students are conditioned not to trust the validity of what they perceive to be meaningful experiences, they begin to feel alienated from such experiences in a manner that suggests to them that those experiences may be frivolous and not worth pursuing. In other words, they are actually learning to regard their own experiences of their world as being less worthwhile than the experiences that others who have been placed in charge of the direction of their learning have decided they should be having.

This mistrust, which is often engendered in students in today's schools, is the result of our need as educators for certainty. That is, we are so intensely eager that young people acquire particular skills and knowledge at specific ages that we insist on controlling their educational environments by beginning with a false premise—that, as an educator, one must necessarily structure students' learning situations for them in advance of their experiences in order to ensure that significant learning takes place.

We need to know exactly what method or approach we can employ to produce certain predetermined results before we can trust that young people's learning will not become random and chaotic. In our quest for certainty, we fail to realize the danger that any sort of predetermined method or approach might easily become an invisible barrier that prevents students from completing their own experiences. Rigidly setting up a learning environment in advance of students' experiences of it inevitably leads toward a lack of genuine contact between the students' individual experiences and the particulars of the specific milieus in which they find themselves.

On a surface level, this incomplete experience is often manifested by little more than a disappointed look on a young person's face when compelled to leave something behind that is engaging for something else that is less interesting, when denied the opportunity to attempt closer relations with peers because of a rigid daily schedule, or when not permitted to pursue certain impressions that are germinating within to their fullest possible fruition due to cognition-based learning that is introduced to achieve certain predetermined results.

However, on a deeper level, something far more dangerous is taking place. What also often occurs is that young people experience a lack of fulfillment, a sense of incompletion in regard to the experiences that they wish to pursue. They begin to sense that there should necessarily be a boundary imposed by others on where their experience might take them. Consequently, they begin to hesitate before taking their experiences to a point of completion because they have now become hesitant to do so.

This hesitation may be a matter of someone who only superficially investigates a topic because he or she believes that it is not possible to go into it any deeper on his or her own. Or it may manifest itself in a student who feels that certain learning activities in which he or she is engaged have little or no meaning because they

CHAPTER 1

are not part of an adult-sanctioned curriculum. However, the mistrustfulness of their own experiences with rigidly preconceived approaches, which are today increasingly imposed on young people in order to achieve certain empirical results, are in many cases going to condition students to grow toward adulthood with a decided uncertainty about their own curiosities and impulses.

In considering these matters, contemporary educators would be well served to realize that there is indeed an inevitable choice to be made. On the one hand, there is results-driven learning, aimed at achieving the best possible external validations of student learning vis-à-vis various tests of their abilities, standardized or otherwise. On the other hand, there is a more experiential approach that gives the healthy evolution of young people's experience (i.e., the manner in which they make increasing contact with their world) a primary place of importance.

Although the essential difference between results-oriented and process-oriented types of learning are addressed in chapter 2 concerning learning and personal experience, for now it seems important to consider the following: If teachers can ultimately engender meaningful learning by beginning with healthy experiential dynamics, can they also fully synthesize these two things if they begin with external results and then make those the fulcrum of young people's learning?

Once one introduces learning programs based primarily on achieving certain empirical results, a process of disembodied experience would seem to be inevitably initiated in the students who are being educated according to these. This, too, will be addressed more specifically in the chapters that follow, particularly with respect to evaluations and disembodied learning in chapter 3.

Unfortunately, particularly now that school funding is so inextricably tied to scores on standardized tests, the present results-driven culture, initiated primarily by the ironically named No

## OUR RESULTS-DRIVEN TESTING CULTURE

Child Left Behind program, has become a thoroughly entrenched reality. Increasingly one hears educators refer to successful schools and optimal learning in terms of student test scores and, at the same time, less and less in terms of the individual experience of students as they learn.

In addition, and what is extremely deleterious, is that the desire by schools and educators to produce the highest possible scores on standardized tests is now determining the nature of actual curriculums that many schools employ in order to produce these scores. In other words, evaluative procedures themselves have now become part and parcel of actual curriculum development. Whole curriculums are now often planned merely to ensure certain quantifiable results that were decided in advance students should be expected to produce in order to demonstrate what they have learned.

This sort of teaching-to-the-test mentality that now invades many of our schools is a complete inversion of the proper relationship between student learning and any diagnostic procedures that teachers might use to assess that learning. If used in a natural, healthy manner, evaluative procedures should be employed by educators to assess the strengths and weaknesses of students so that the adult can then provide the young person with more effective, intelligent direction. To use these sorts of evaluations to instead create the very areas that students learn, and how they learn them, sends a powerful negative message to the young person that the whole point of learning is to simply please other people.

It also means that many educators and schools are now saying to parents whose continued confidence they are trying to ensure, "We know how your child can best learn because we can teach him how to be successful at the measure we have designed to evaluate that learning." Needless to say, this sort of cart-before-the-horse, circular, nonsensical approach ensures the inevitability

## CHAPTER 1

of student learning being carefully compelled in whatever direction leads toward the greatest degree of success at such external measures of validation, rather than evolving naturally from the student's own curiosities and impulses.

Our schools should have a deeper purpose than one of simply preparing students for achieving success on a purely external level. They should be primarily involved with how the experiences of individual students evolve as those students approach and become engaged by specific subject matters and by their learning environment itself. Unless that vital connection between a young person's learning and his or her individual experience is allowed to remain intact, then neither the learning nor the experience is developing as it should. Rather, what is transpiring, as much as anything, is that young minds are being conditioned to traverse well-worn paths in the name of school funding and adult accountability.

The chapters that follow are an attempt to simply examine how a primarily results-driven approach to learning will affect the personal experiences of young people in their formative years in unhealthy ways. It is not a social study based on data about learning and curriculum development; that will be left for other books on this subject that hopefully will be written.

Rather, it is a thought-provoking examination of the natural relationship that exists between learning and personal experience, and how those two processes can evolve in young people in both healthy and unhealthy ways as they are being educated. In this regard, it is intended for parents, teachers, students, and anyone concerned with the state of contemporary education who is interested in examining how academic learning and personal experience might remain fused in the student as a singular, healthy, holistic process.

# 2

# LEARNING AND EXPERIENCE

In most schools today, learning progressions in different subject areas are becoming ever more predetermined. It is inevitable that if teachers are increasingly under the gun, so to speak, they will feel the need to be ever more in control of the learning progressions that those students employ in order to be certain that their students perform well on various standardized tests. Of course, at the same time, in conjunction with this increased scrutiny, teachers have become ever more watchful of learners who might be moving away from the information, knowledge, and skills that have been determined will give students the best chance to assimilate subject matter from a predetermined, results-driven curriculum.

However, much as one accepts the fact that this is simply the way things are in many of today's schools, there is still one important question that needs to be asked, one that seems not to be asked nearly enough: What happens when the specific direction that the teacher has determined for the student's learning begins to move in a different direction from where the student's own

# CHAPTER 2

curiosities and interests lead him or her? Does one ignore those curiosities and interests in order to proceed with the preconceived learning path, or does one dispense with this path in order to follow the student's own tendencies?

This was certainly a question that had to be dealt with every day at The Children's School. In fact, this was true particularly because the students there were given the sort of latitude in creating their own lessons plans that they would most likely not be given in more traditional schools. The issue of allowing them to gravitate toward what naturally attracted them, in lieu of staying entirely focused on subject areas and lessons for which they had agreed to be responsible, came up repeatedly.

Often, this would take the form of students who were working in a particular area of science, art, or geography suddenly coming upon something that was not part of the original lesson and that they wanted to discuss at length with one of the teachers. This led to the inevitable question of what was more important: the inner discipline of remaining with the particular subject matter the student was assimilating or focusing on something new that had piqued his or her interest.

Of course, many educators will say that the obvious answer is to simply take time to assimilate the student's interests into the preconceived area of study, and often that is quite possible to accomplish. One can do this if the curriculum is somehow broad enough to include any related interests and if the learning environment is flexible enough to allow for learning on a more individual basis.

However, there is yet a larger question here that transcends the mere conflict between a student's interest in a singular subject and the specific areas of prescribed curriculum that do not necessarily include that subject. This involves the direction of a learning path that the students themselves have no control over and how this particular lack of control will affect the future relationships between young persons' personal experiences and their learning. If the teacher, rather than the students, has exclusive control over the direction that specific learning progressions take, it seems almost impossible to assume that the students will remain fully anchored in their own experiences as they learn.

If young people are to be fully connected to what they are learning, it seems essential that they play a significant role in creating the particular paths by which they approach a certain area of knowledge. Today's schools, however, seem to continually violate this basic principle and, in so doing, sever the potential organic link between learning and personal experience. This they do when they impose on their students a predetermined curriculum leading toward preconceived validations of learning that rule out from their inception the possibility that students will have any real say in developing the progression that they are employing to learn certain subject matter.

At The Children's School, students were allowed to negotiate their own approaches to various subject matter for which they had agreed to be responsible. In determining these, by sitting down with students individually or occasionally within the context of a small group, the responsibility of the teacher was to assist the student in developing a plan for approaching a particular subject area. In doing this, there was the constant, often very difficult balancing act of developing workable learning paths in acquiring certain knowledge and information, yet ones in which the aim was that the students would feel that it was "their" learning paths that were being created.

Yet, when this worked, as it did when teachers who were familiar enough with a particular student were able to introduce certain aspects of it that they knew would intrigue him or her, it often eliminated much of the usual "tug-of-war" in getting students to learn simply because their learning was now stemming directly from their unique perceptions of the particular subject area.

Obviously, this approach is very different from the standard approach employed in many schools today, in which students learn a subject by being asked to assimilate predetermined curricula that they have had no real hand in creating. Whereas, by giving young people a greater hand in determining the path by which they approach a particular subject, based on their unique interests and the particular point of view that they might have developed toward the subject, the students are given the opportunity to learn the subject from the inside out by organically creating the path by which they approach it.

On the other hand, when a curriculum is employed that is entirely predetermined and results oriented, students are simply adhering to something that is being created in advance by someone else. As a consequence, their experience of what they are learning will be primarily one of trying to accommodate themselves to a progression that actually exists outside of them. Their learning becomes a step-by-step process that does not originate with their direct experience of the subject matter but begins with the need to adapt to a preconceived curriculum for the purpose of attaining certain empirical results that they are told are synonymous with becoming a successful learner.

The difference between these two approaches, the organic progression that originates with the student's own experience of a particular subject matter and the established curriculum that originates with a teacher's preconceptions concerning the subject, is nothing short of fundamental. The first permits personal experience and learning to be bound together as one continuous process. The latter effectively severs what should be an inherent relationship connecting the two by causing students to experience their learning as a process that exists outside of them in a disembodied fashion.

If students are working with their teacher to determine the direction that a particular learning progression might take, then their direct experience of the subject and their learning are synonymous simply because they are both moving in the same direction. As students make informed choices, assisted by their teacher, as to where they want to move next in acquiring certain skills, information, or knowledge, the students' learning of a subject is proceeding directly from their own experience of it.

On the other hand, if the direction that their learning is going to take has already been determined by those adults who have prepared the approach to a subject for them in advance, then the learning progression that those young people employ exists outside of them, even though they are assimilating it as their own. The students' comprehension of the particular subject matter originates somewhere else, outside of their own experience of trying to come to grips with it.

For learning and personal experience to be bound together in the student—particularly for a child—as one continuous process, his or her learning must originate with direct experience of the knowledge or skills that he or she is attempting to acquire. Otherwise, if that knowledge or those skills are coming to the student secondhand through an entirely preplanned curriculum, rather than by the young person becoming acquainted with them by assimilating them through a learning progression of which he or she has a significant measure of control, the student's learning is no longer originating with his or her own experience. Instead, it is now a process to be assimilated as his or her own even though it originated entirely outside of the student.

Furthermore, this separation of learning from direct experience becomes increasingly calcified as the young person moves toward adulthood. Eventually, young people come to see learning as something that they "do" rather than something that they "are." When this occurs, they have reached the point where their

CHAPTER 2

experience as they learn will probably never fully feel to them like their own simply because it is no longer something that they are able to willfully control, as they would if it had begun with their interests, curiosities, and tendencies.

Consequently, a habitual pattern has been set up in students in which the strength of their impressions as they learn becomes significantly dulled and diluted simply because their learning, rather than originating with their own curiosities and impulses, is now more of an external process that they simply follow, much as one follows directions on a map. As a result, the subject matter that they are attempting to assimilate is always going to be one step removed from them simply because the direction by which they are approaching it is perpetually originating outside of them. Yes, of course, they may readily acquire certain skills and knowledge— however, this acquisition will have come at the cost of being fully connected to the areas of learning with which they are engaging.

On the other hand, if the students' learning actually originates with their own personal experiences because they are continually creating the path by which they approach a specific subject matter, then that learning will actually become part of them in a way that it possibly couldn't if it had evolved according to a pre-planned, results-driven curriculum.

This was something that I and other teachers were able to observe on an ongoing basis—this sense of ownership that occurs in young people when they know they are in control of the direction of their learning. Sometimes this involved working with a student individually on learning a certain basic skill—learning to write a complete sentence or learning to carry figures between numerical hierarchies, for example—and taking time to respond to questions of "why" he or she needed to focus on certain aspects of it. Other times, it was a matter of listening to student suggestions as to what direction a small group lesson on great scientific discoveries or constitutional law might take.

## LEARNING AND EXPERIENCE

However, because of things such as time constraints, the necessity of working with another student, or a lack of patience by a certain teacher on a particular day, there were times when we weren't able to effectively respond to these questions or suggestions. Then, it was often possible to actually see and feel the students' learning and full involvement begin to separate. One could watch them return to their lessons with the same dispirited, accusing look that classroom teachers everywhere observe when lessons with their students become too predetermined and compulsory.

By employing these sorts of predetermined, compulsory approaches to subject matters that they hope will lead toward certain empirical results, educators everywhere are ensuring that this same unhealthy split between learning and personal experience is going to take place. On the other hand, by working with students to develop learning progressions that can directly connect them to various subject areas because those progressions have evolved from the students' own interests and unique points of view toward these subjects, educators are facilitating learning and personal experience that are being bound together as a singular, healthy movement.

If one actually agrees with giving young people a greater voice in the direction that their learning might take, the obvious next question is one of how to change our classrooms so that this can actually occur. Unless the environments themselves in which students learn become less results oriented and more experientially based, it will be impossible to realistically involve those students in the creation of their own learning progressions and approaches to different subject matters.

This was a luxury we had given ourselves at The Children's School when it was announced at the first organizational meeting to create the school that we would give no grades and would not require students to take any standardized tests, unless they asked to do so. Because there was no pressure to produce the empirical results that would please parents, school boards, or the public at large, there could be a genuine dialogue with students about the direction of their learning.

Sometimes, of course, this became extremely frustrating. This was particularly true when students were generally unmotivated, had become too accustomed to their parents or teachers from other schools directing them too obtrusively, or when they had such a limited idea of a particular subject area that they just weren't able to effectively make their own choices. However, when this process of students creating their own learning paths worked, it was often possible for teachers to be able to experience themselves simply as knowledgeable children working with other children to investigate the world—a moment that nearly all classroom teachers of students in their formative years will be able to recognize as being among the very best.

However, the way in which most contemporary learning environments are now conceived and constructed works entirely against this more inclusive approach; the main impediment is, of course, the approaches to learning that are almost entirely results oriented rather than process oriented in the correct manner. That is to say, the important principles that assist us as educators in intelligently guiding the learning process in young minds need to evolve primarily from the curiosities, interests, and impressions of individual students rather than from our need to produce predetermined results by ignoring those sorts of experiential dynamics.

In the past, there has been a real dichotomy in education between results-oriented and process-oriented learning. In point of fact, many educators see these two approaches as being mutually exclusive when this is not necessarily the case. Process learning, if correctly conceived, focuses primarily on how the learner connects with skills or information that he or she is attempting to assimilate, while results-oriented learning tends to focus much more on how proficiently the learner has acquired the new knowledge or skills.

Of course, many educators who believe in a more results-oriented approach think that the problem with process-oriented learning is simply that it tends to focus too much on the comfort level of the learner as he or she is making contact with new skills or new information, rather than how competently he or she is doing so.

For example, a typical criticism by an educator who believes in a more results-oriented approach to learning to write well is that process-oriented approaches spend too much time on personal areas such as the interests that the students are developing while learning to write or on the degree to which they can tie their writing to their speech. Those critics believe the focus should be more on developing the concrete ability to put coherent ideas into complete sentences with proper grammar and syntax.

However, even though it seems logical to assume that these two approaches are inevitably at variance with one another, this certainly does not have to be the case. True process-oriented learning, because it factors in the actual dynamics of a student's experience, will in fact lead to more complete learning. A true process-oriented approach begins with the supposition that personal experience and academic learning are both part of the same experiential flow.

Meaningful learning occurs best when learners have the opportunity to take their curiosities and impressions to a point of completion. Otherwise, they may be merely digesting facts, information, and skills given them by someone else in which they have no genuine interest, and on which they have no real perspective.

For example, if a child who is studying basic genetics simply learns what DNA is and what it does, then learns where it is located in the human cell, then learns how genetic mutations occur,

CHAPTER 2

and so forth and so on, that child is simply learning a sequence of facts that do not necessarily permit him or her to genuinely experience what he or she is trying to comprehend. The only thing that will really allow students to do this is to permit them to follow a particular aspect of the subject matter that genuinely intrigues them—for instance, how exactly a mutation in a certain species occurs—until the student feels that he or she has followed that interest to the point where it begins to open up the rest of the learning area to him or her.

This is exactly what occurred when a group of four students between the ages of seven and eleven expressed an interest in genetics and DNA to me. In particular, they wanted to know more about the sorts of mutations that might cause someone to be born with six fingers, albino hair, or a predisposition to getting cancer. By following this interest steadily forward, using only the students' increasing interest in something with which they had become acquainted to determine a learning path, we moved steadily from different types of mutations in both people and various animals to how mutations actually occur in the structure of someone's DNA.

Eventually, the four students and I were able, using a text in organic chemistry, to construct a small strand of the DNA molecule by using different-colored gumdrops representing atoms to build the four chemical bases that have to be put together correctly if no genetic mutations are to occur. We did this by simply moving from one natural interest to the next. Nothing more.

This is what involving students in the creation of their own learning progressions does. It connects them to areas of learning as a whole, rather than causing them to become familiar with a particular subject matter in a much more restrictive manner in which they tend to only acquire isolated bits of information. When young people have worked to not only develop specific points of view toward the knowledge they are assimilating but also have had a significant hand in creating the actual approaches that allow them to acquire that knowledge, their understanding of the entire subject matter becomes much more complete.

This is also why process-oriented approaches to learning, which focus initially on how students might come fully into contact with what they are endeavoring to learn, will in the long run produce more complete, long-lasting learning. Approaches that focus exclusively on making sure that students acquire highly specific information and skills by compelling those students to adhere to predetermined curricula, however, will primarily produce short-term learning in which students are not as fully connected to the subject matter they are assimilating.

It is certainly possible for educators to develop learning environments that allow young people to learn in a more meaningful manner than they do in the majority of today's schools. The key, however, is to involve students from the beginning in the creation of progressions by which they approach various subject matters so that their learning will consequently proceed from the inside out. Yet, in order to do this, we must begin to give up the false premise that a young person's competent acquisition of knowledge and skills requires that his or her teacher control in advance the manner in which that acquisition takes place to achieve certain preconceived results.

Unfortunately, in our present results-driven culture in which standardized test scores and good grades are becoming ever more the very definitions of what successful learning implies, we are moving increasingly away from this. In fact, in many of our schools today, both public and private, we are in real danger of instituting a codified culture in which students are given the message that one learns solely in order to achieve certain results that will please other people in positions of authority. Then, if and when this occurs, we will have at last reached the point where we

## CHAPTER 2

have genuinely caused the separation of learning from personal experience in many of the young people whom we educate.

Again, if students lose control of the paths by which they approach various knowledge, information, and skills because of the need by educators to achieve certain empirical results, then their learning will be increasingly experienced by them as a disembodied process that necessarily exists outside of them. Consequently, not only will their impressions, curiosities, and impulses be dulled by this, but they will also habitually begin to judge their own ability to investigate different aspects of their world according to the messages that have been given them by others about themselves. As a result, their initiative in pursuing certain interests will often be stifled.

Also, if a significant portion of young people's school days is devoted to preparing them to perform well on standardized tests by instructing them according to a curriculum that leads toward better test performance, or even simply preparing them to actually take these tests, there is inevitably going to be little time left for assisting them in developing a workable point of view toward what they are learning. Consequently, it will not be possible for them to develop enough of a perspective on various subject matters to become competent enough to develop their own learning progressions, both in terms of the larger world outside of school and in terms of their own interests and tendencies.

In addition, the subject matter of most standardized tests does not begin to reflect the rate of rapid change that is now so prevalent within our culture in so many different areas. Therefore, those curriculums that are developed primarily to facilitate the highest possible scores on tests end up being severely limited by the actual subject matter of the tests themselves. As a result, students' awareness of the possibilities inherent in a particular subject matter, both in terms of its potential scope and its possible relation to a particular student's unique interests, becomes acutely restricted.

We can no longer cling to the notion that the individual experience of young people as they approach different areas of learning is significantly less important than how successful they are at acquiring skills and knowledge according to predetermined plans that allow them to reproduce these things. Should we do so, we will continue to engender learning in students in which their initiative is stifled and their personal experience is dulled.

There are indeed ways to ascertain whether or not students are learning that do not do this sort of damage to their inner lives. Some of these will be dealt with in chapter 3, which concerns evaluations and disembodied learning. However, for now it seems important to say that today's educators need to be ever watchful of how exactly young people's learning actually evolves. If it evolves primarily from adult preconceptions aimed at producing certain empirical results, then there is the distinct danger that the personal experience and learning of students will begin to inexorably separate from each other as they learn in an increasingly disinterested manner.

# EVALUATIONS AND DISEMBODIED LEARNING

Grades, and tests leading toward grades, have become so much a part of what we think of as education that, for many, it is almost impossible to think of any approach to young people's learning that does not, by its very nature, include them. Grades and tests have become almost synonymous with how well a student has learned. Most people believe that without these sorts of evaluations by which we can measure the progress of students in their formative years, it is not really possible to get a good grip on how much learning is in fact transpiring.

Rooted in the entrenchment of these external, comparative standards is the fundamental idea that one can ascertain what a student is accomplishing only by comparing that student's learning with the learning of other students. Part and parcel of all this is the notion that a student cannot know how well he or she is progressing unless there is some sort of judgmental measure attached to his or her learning.

Granted, if it is important that contemporary education be primarily concerned with this judgmental, comparative approach in

# CHAPTER 3

which one learns in order to garner some sort of extrinsic reward, then grades, tests, and other similar evaluations have a valid place within the context of this particular outlook. However, if one believes that learning must always, by its very nature, remain an essentially intrinsic endeavor in which one's curiosity should be the very entity that not only drives the entire process but also determines its very direction, then these sorts of external evaluations should have, at best, a marginal place in how young people are educated.

To manipulate students through grades and tests into learning something in which they might not otherwise be interested, or to make second person's judgments on how much of a specific subject area they have properly assimilated, is to take the impetus and will to learn something for its own sake away from the young person and replace it with a reason for learning that has almost nothing to do with the actual learning itself.

A student who has a genuine interest in a particular area of learning is given periodic tests to see how much of the relevant knowledge he or she has learned. The student is then given a letter grade or score based on how well he or she did on those tests. Very likely, if this student responds in the manner in which most young people respond to grades and tests, the letter grade or score he or she receives will soon become as important, or more important, to the student than his or her original curiosity about the particular subject area.

Unfortunately, the messages sent to young people by grades, or by tests that lead to grades, so strongly affect their own sense of themselves as effective or ineffective learners that these types of evaluations usually become the primary impetus that determines the students' motivation to learn. As a result, the major source of a student's involvement in his or her learning becomes one of undertaking this learning for some reason that is periph-

## EVALUATIONS AND DISEMBODIED LEARNING

eral to the learning itself, thus causing the student to be outside of it in disembodied fashion.

Then, once this begins to occur, students are already well on their way to not becoming fully engaged by, or connected to, the objects of their learning. Instead, they are attempting to connect with areas of learning for reasons that are completely unrelated to what might be their own natural interests in these areas.

The dangers of severing the connection between a young person's natural interests and why he or she undertakes any type of learning simply cannot be overstated. First of all, for learning to be meaningful to students in their formative years, it must involve their entire persona—their curiosities, their natural interests, their individual feel for the subject matter, as much as it involves their purely cognitive processes. Learning that is undertaken for some reason that is exterior to these things soon resides less and less within the world of the student's tendencies, enthusiasms, and emotional investments. Rather, it becomes very much a mental game in which the prizes are good grades and adult evaluations, which are dangled in front of the student like the proverbial carrot that is dangled in front of the horse to keep him moving in the right direction.

As a consequence of this separation of their interests and curiosities from the reasons why they are learning something, young people often come to feel that learning is inherently a process that is exterior to what is occurring within their own hearts and minds, rather than something that germinates primarily within themselves. Over time, they come to experience their learning as an increasingly disembodied mental process that is distinct from their curiosities, interests, and impulses.

Once students in their formative years begin to feel that learning, by its very nature, is a process that exists outside of them, they can also easily begin to feel that they must necessarily

# CHAPTER 3

depend on the experience and expertise of others in order to truly learn something, rather than be able to follow their own direction in doing so. When this begins to occur, students are already well on their way, at an early stage of life, toward becoming compromised people who must necessarily inherit their views of the world from others, rather than attempting to draw them out of their own experiences.

During the time The Children's School was in existence, this was an issue that had to be dealt with repeatedly. Students who had spent a significant amount of time in other schools came to the school heavily conditioned by grades and test scores; they believed that unless there was some sort of external validation of their learning, given them by their teachers, there was really no point in undertaking such learning.

In fact, some of the older students, who had been in more traditional, results-driven schools for a long time before they came to us, weren't able to actually perceive the learning environment in which they now found themselves. That is, they often just didn't get it that they were now in an environment where they could have genuine control of their learning if that was what they wanted. Many times, they would ask one of the teachers exactly what they would get if they learned some aspect of a certain subject or completed a particular personal project. In other words, they had already been so conditioned by the external validations of their learning, or lack of them, they had received at other schools that they had lost nearly all sense of learning something simply because they were interested in doing so.

The inherent danger of giving young people grades is something far more severe than simply the risk of deflating a student's confidence and initiative with poor marks, although that is also an important consideration. The real danger is that grades and other similar adult evaluations often initiate an irreversible separation in the young person of personal experience from learning.

## EVALUATIONS AND DISEMBODIED LEARNING

Let's say a certain student becomes interested in learning a particular subject matter. He finds that he has a great degree of facility in learning it, and he is also highly interested in the subject area itself. However, before long, his teacher decides to test him on his newfound abilities in this area, and to attach a letter grade to how well he has done on the test. After taking the test, the student finds that he has done very well indeed and receives the top grade possible. Feeling emboldened by this external validation of something that he feels he has a real knack for, the student plunges ahead with the particular subject matter. However, after another brief period of time has passed, his teacher presents him with another test of his abilities, and this time the student receives a lesser grade.

The student continues his study of the subject matter, but now his interest in it is no longer just a matter of his natural curiosity about it. Now he has an external reason to learn it: to prove to himself, and to his teacher, that his knowledge of, and ability in, the particular area of learning have not diminished, that they are just as great as they were when he originally received the top grade for his efforts.

Consequently, the student now has an ulterior motive for learning the subject, a motive that is completely exterior to his own curiosities and interests. This motive, of course, is knowing enough about it to receive a top grade on the next exam. Such an external motive will nearly always diminish the student's original curious interest in, and strong feeling for, a certain area of learning. Instead, it will significantly replace these with a need to accomplish something related to the subject area in order to receive the particular external validation that the student is after.

This is true simply because it is impossible for these two things—intense, curious interest in something for its own sake and the need to receive some sort of external validation of one's capacities—to exist simultaneously. Once one has even a minimal

CHAPTER 3

need to receive some sort of external validation of what one is learning, then one's focus in learning that something will inevitably be shaped by the need to acquire whatever capacities give one that particular validation. In other words, the natural flow of the student's learning will almost certainly be shaped by the need to follow whichever path will most easily and effectively lead toward the particular external reward.

Once that occurs, this shaping of the direction of one's learning in order to receive a certain grade or score, then the intensity of interest in the particular subject area is going to be inevitably diminished. Working to achieve some sort of external approval for learning something is going to inherently shape the path of that learning, whereas maintaining one's intensity of interest while learning requires that the approach one is using takes place in a completely open-ended fashion that allows for any sudden twists and turns that might occur along the way.

In other words, once students who are learning a certain subject become concerned with receiving some sort of external validation for their efforts, such as a grade, they are going to automatically, almost imperceptibly, begin to steer the flow of their learning in the direction of whichever path gives them the best chance of attaining the desired external reward. If they know that focusing on a certain area of a subject matter is important because it will become more of a focal point for how their learning will be evaluated than other areas will, they are most likely going to be more concerned with that particular area, even though it might not have been what in fact drew them toward the subject matter in the first place.

Now any feelings of genuine personal connection to the specific area of learning that students may have experienced when they first encountered it have been diminished. In their place is the need to follow a certain path toward the subject matter that might not be what they are genuinely interested in but will give

## EVALUATIONS AND DISEMBODIED LEARNING

them the best chance for success with external validations of their learning. Consequently, there is evolving within students a false understanding that learning is inherently a matter of adhering to something that exists outside of them, independent of what they might be interested in from one moment to the next. When this point has been completely reached, learning will very likely begin to feel to young people as if it were a process that no longer truly belongs to them.

In addition to creating in the students this disembodied feeling toward their learning, the grades, tests, and other evaluations also tend to initiate a dulling of their experiences. There is a good reason why, as young people proceed down the road of their school experience, many seem to become not as interested in what might possibly engage them. The impressions of many of them also appear to become markedly less vivid. In large measure, the reason for this isn't just the normal growth process and growing more used to life in the world. It also happens because their experience is growing more dulled because they are continually and habitually redirecting it in order to measure up to the external standards that the adults who run their schools have created for them.

Again, this was something that we were able to observe any number of times in students who came to our school from more traditional ones where grades and standardized tests had been very much a part of their world. There was often a certain dullness in their attitude toward lessons and learning when juxtaposed against the general attitude toward these things by students who had always been at our school and so had never known these sorts of external devices for judging their learning.

Admittedly, the level of academic competence of our students wasn't always at or above that of the students who had come from more traditional learning environments, yet there was an eagerness in our group that many of the new students seemed not to

## CHAPTER 3

possess. And when our school worked for these new students, it was gratifying to see this same eagerness begin to grow in them.

For young people's experiences to remain sharply alive for them as they learn, it is vitally important that they be allowed to take learning to a point of completion, rather than having to continually interrupt it because they feel compelled to direct it along a particular path in order to receive some sort of external validation. Students who develop particular interests as they are learning a certain subject matter need to be given the time and space to fully assimilate these interests in the sort of impressionistic manner that will allow their experience to remain vivid.

Influencing where the students direct their attention with grades and tests is going to inherently cause them to merely skate along the surface of a subject matter because they feel compelled to direct it along a particular path. As a consequence, the original power and clarity of impressions that might have evolved from their natural curiosities and interests will almost certainly become dulled.

In other words, for students in their formative years to be fully involved in their learning so that their interests and impressions retain their original level of intensity, they need to feel that they are in control of the direction of such learning. Otherwise, they will end up directing their attention to places where their natural curiosity is not inclined to go, and their experiences themselves will tend to grow less vivid than they might potentially be.

External devices such as grades, which are deeply manipulative, have the effect of removing this feeling of control that young people might otherwise have over their own experiences as they learn simply because they influence the students to direct their attention in certain directions in order to receive adult acknowledgments that they are becoming successful learners. As a result, students are often not able to directly connect with a particular area of learning according to their unique experiences of it.

## EVALUATIONS AND DISEMBODIED LEARNING

Rather, they are connecting with that learning on someone else's terms so that they can then be rewarded for doing so.

Certainly it is possible for adults to assist young people with their learning and to even provide them with reliable, relevant feedback without the use of grades, tests, and other adult-generated evaluative procedures. The answer lies in understanding why these sorts of manipulative devices exist in the first place. Most of the time they exist to motivate students who are unmotivated to learn a particular subject primarily because they are given such a limited amount of information about the entire context in which the subject exists.

Young people, even young children, usually understand what information and skills they are expected to assimilate, and they usually have a pretty good idea of how well they are expected to assimilate them. Beyond these two basic things, however, they are often highly unaware of the entire milieu in which the knowledge that they are assimilating actually occurs and of exactly how it might become more interesting to them.

Take the case of a student who is learning the subject of algebra for the first time. For her to possess a firm sense of the entire subject matter, she needs to become familiar with a number of different things. One, she needs to have developed a relatively good idea of what algebra is. For instance, is it just a matter of combining different numerical and symbolic values in an assortment of various combinations, or does it really represent a certain implied order in the real world itself? In other words, to really understand algebra, the student needs to know what concrete realities it might actually represent. An obvious part of this understanding might in fact be the history of algebra—how it originally came into being and what purpose it serves.

In addition, for the subject of algebra to have any real meaning for the young person who is studying it, she needs to know exactly how to make use of it—not only in her immediate daily life

## CHAPTER 3

but also how she might use it during the course of her future interests, and even possible careers, as she grows toward adulthood. Finally, she needs to have a clear idea of the exact learning sequence upon which she is embarking in her study of algebra. She needs to know what information and skills lie just down the road so that she can have a clear understanding of why what she is learning might be significant later on.

If the student has a clear understanding of these things, then she has a much better chance of intrinsically understanding not only the possible attractiveness and significance of learning algebra but also why it might be a meaningful area of study for her. If after her teacher has assisted her in making these things clearer to herself, she still has very little or no interest in learning algebra, attempting to motivate her extrinsically, with grades and test scores, probably isn't going to make much difference anyway. She may well become acquainted with the subject, but it will be an acquaintance without any genuine, lasting meaning for her.

Our systems of education have become heavily reliant on adult-generated evaluations of learning to motivate students simply because young people often have an unclear picture of why they are expected to engage in certain types of learning. If, before introducing students to a particular subject, their teachers spent significant time familiarizing them with not only the basic history of the subject matter but also what they could potentially gain by studying it, then genuine efforts could most likely be made to motivate students naturally and intrinsically from within, rather than through the often contrived manipulations of grades and tests.

This was something with which we struggled repeatedly in attempting to introduce certain subject matter—such as algebra, particular periods of history, or certain sciences—by giving them a genuine purpose. Yet, while doing so, we also knew full well that a significant part of the reason these subjects were being introduced was to prepare students for the middle or high school they would be next attending. The students would often want to know the exact reasons for learning these things, and many times the best answer that could be given to them was that they needed to know them for freshman year in the local high school, which was, of course, not an adequate answer for most of them. Consequently, upon hearing this, on occasion students would begin to actually lose interest in the particular subject.

Unfortunately, at this point, the rigid, predetermined curriculums that one often finds in American secondary schools began to creep into our little school. In the end, it's very difficult, if not impossible, to keep the world outside from entering the schoolhouse door, sometimes in ways that make the administration of a democratic school much more challenging.

Surely it is possible to give young people appropriate feedback on how well they are learning in a nonjudgmental fashion. The answer lies in simply showing them, when they have made mistakes, where they may have gone wrong and then allowing them to remain focused on acquiring certain knowledge or mastering a particular skill until they feel comfortable that they have done so.

Testing and grading them on how well they have done these things is, by force of human nature, only going to cause them to work their psyches into the well-worn ruts that they know in advance will allow them to do well on these kinds of evaluations. The long-term result is often the development in them of the misunderstanding that the correct path to making genuine contact with a particular area of learning lies inherently outside of both the subject matter and the learning situation itself.

The correct approach to educating students in their formative years, if it is anything, needs to be a process that takes pains to allow their motivation to learn something and the subject matter to remain intrinsically connected. That is to say, the reasons a young person might be interested in a particular area of learning lie

## CHAPTER 3

within that area of learning itself. The area might contain a natural interest that the student has already developed, it might be something in the student's life that naturally attracts him or her, it might allow the student to develop specific skills or acquire certain knowledge that he or she understands is needed, or it might permit the student to connect more fully with his or her learning environment and with other people in it.

Three twelve-year-old boys at The Children's School began learning fairly advanced theoretical physics, and eventually attended a lecture on imaginary time by Stephen Hawking, simply because they became fascinated with the idea that gravity is an actual warping of the fabric of space and wanted to know more about this.

A thirteen-year-old girl worked diligently on her math skills simply because she didn't want to be embarrassed about these when she entered high school the next year. Another younger child wanted to learn to write better so she could attend one of the weekly writers' conferences, at which a group of students visited one of the local coffee houses to drink hot chocolate or coffee while they read their stories, poems, or short plays to each other. All of these are examples in which the motivation to learn something was entirely intrinsic to the subject matter or learning situation itself.

In other words, if any of these intrinsic reasons for learning not only exists but is also made clear to a student, then it is indeed possible for that student to be motivated to learn because he or she has a reason to do so that is intrinsic to the subject matter itself. Motivating the student to learn extrinsically by placing the reasons to learn before him or her in the form of grades and test scores, however, is inevitably going to significantly prevent that student from discovering for himself or herself that the true motivation to learn something always lies with the actual area of learning itself.

Then, once the external motivations begin to occur, which they nearly always will simply because young people tend to be so easily influenced by the possibility of adult approval, students will then begin to inevitably look for the motivation to learn in the form of some sort of extrinsic reward that they can be given for learning, not within the area of learning itself. The obvious danger of this is that they will then begin to spend less time and energy in determining for themselves why a particular area of learning might be interesting to them. Then, as this becomes an increasingly entrenched habit, they will begin connecting with different subject areas on a much more superficial level.

To fully connect with a particular area of learning, it is essential that students develop the capacity to comprehend exactly why the particular area might actually be interesting to them. Otherwise, it is just knowledge and information that they are attempting to digest without genuinely understanding why they are doing so.

The manner in which most of today's schools operate makes it very difficult to motivate students without the use of grades and tests simply because students have become so thoroughly reliant upon external standards for confirmation that they are indeed learning. Yet, at the same time, these same external validations of learning have been derived from a false premise concerning what true accountability for learning really means. True accountability is always a matter of personal, not external, accountability.

External accountability means measuring up to external standards and judgments that one has had no hand in creating. For example, an individual student receiving good grades or the students in a particular teacher's class scoring well on a standardized test means only that students and teacher have focused their attention and behavior in a certain direction in order to reproduce information, knowledge, or skills for which they did not necessarily agree beforehand to be responsible. This is not true accountability simply because it does not involve students and teachers themselves setting the parameters for which they are going to be accountable.

On the other hand, personal accountability means that there is an actual agreement made between teacher and student concerning what each is taking responsibility for. For instance, a teacher is obviously responsible for following through on such things as providing significant materials and resources, devoting certain periods of time each day to teaching a specific subject matter, or providing clear, intelligent sequences for learning. A student is inherently responsible for things like completing agreed-upon work on time, devoting specific periods of the day to attempting to assimilate certain subject matter, or even providing the teacher with appropriate feedback concerning what the student is not comprehending.

True accountability always involves this element of personal responsibility, which means the student has a significant hand in determining the exact details of what his or her responsibility toward learning actually entails. For a teacher to provide an education for the young people in his or her class in which there is this sort of true accountability means simply that the students play an important role in determining that for which they are expected to follow through. For this to occur, grades and test scores, which are exclusively adult-generated measures of success, are indeed counterproductive to students becoming more responsible as they become more accountable.

Such standards of external accountability often serve to remove the reasons it is important for students to be responsible for their learning from the hands of the students simply because they have had no hand in creating those very standards. As a result of this, accountability for learning becomes primarily a matter of digesting facts and information, and also adjusting one's behavior, in order to measure up to somebody else's view of what successful learning is.

The unfortunate consequence of this is that young people are often given a very strong message that the reasons for personal responsibility inherently exist outside their own experience and that personal responsibility begins somewhere in an adult world that they are not yet able to fully comprehend. Therefore, because they are not the people who determine the actual standards to which they need to adjust both their learning and behavior, they are given a highly erroneous picture of what personal responsibility really entails.

That is, the students begin to see personal responsibility as simply acquiescing to the standards of other people who somehow understand acceptable learning and behavior more than the students understand. The very nature of responsibility comes to be seen by young people as simply adhering to the instructions and requirements of other people who are in positions of authority. The students, over time, understand responsible behavior as simply being successful at measuring up to the standards that others who are in this position have determined in advance are important for the students to meet.

This interpretation of responsible behavior begins to instill in the young person's mind the idea that a person is acting responsibly when in fact he or she is actually attempting to act according to standards that someone else has determined are important. Then true personal responsibility—that is, acting on decisions that one has determined for oneself—is instead replaced by the notion that responsible behavior has primarily to do with obediently following the instructions of some external authority.

To send young people the message that they are becoming accountable for their learning when they have had no genuine say either in determining what they are going to learn or in determining the standards by which their learning is going to be judged is very dangerous indeed. It plants in their minds the idea that personal responsibility is primarily a matter of acquiescing to authority, rather than following through on actions for which one has agreed to be responsible.

Therefore, for schools to begin to employ standards of accountability that send students the correct messages concerning what true responsibility should entail means that young people themselves must be given a greater hand in determining their own standards for learning and behavior. In order for this to occur, adult-generated standards such as grades, tests, and test scores must significantly give way to standards of accountability that are more personal in nature.

More specifically, it is important that teachers take the time to work with students on a more individual basis to set standards of learning and behavior that the students themselves have had a significant hand in creating. This can be done by simply working with students to set reasonable goals for learning—and for their conduct in relation to that learning—that can be developed through the creation of learning plans that are acceptable to both student and teacher. Then, after those plans have been developed, both student and teacher should be held accountable for what they said they were going to do.

This occurred at The Children's School whenever a student agreed to take responsibility for learning a specific subject matter or a certain basic skill by a particular point in time, or if a student agreed to meet with a teacher for a certain amount of time each day to work on something he or she had agreed to learn. The teachers were also pretty much held to the same standard. That is, if one of us had agreed to meet with an individual student each day at a certain time to work on something, we needed to be there or else face the student's justifiable dissatisfaction or anger. If we had agreed to provide certain materials for the next day's lessons, we needed to make sure that those materials were either created or bought the night before.

In addition, in establishing these mutual standards of personal accountability between teachers and students, there were ongoing discussions throughout the school day as to who should have certain rights and who should be given certain responsibilities as they pertained to specific learning situations. Sometimes, students would question the fairness of having to hold up their end of the bargain in addressing everything on their individual learning plan when they saw other students, who possessed different capacities and degrees of motivation, asked to be responsible for much less. Other times, teachers would grow frustrated with students when they found themselves putting more time and energy than the students in addressing particular subject matters in which the students had originally expressed an interest.

So, in employing this particular approach to accountability, our standards remained entirely personal. Students were responsible for standards of learning and behavior that they had had a significant hand in creating. As a result, the concept of personal responsibility, with all that it entails, became not only much clearer to all concerned but also much more real, simply because it was something that evolved from actual teacher and student behavior.

Using this approach of personal, rather than external, accountability, it is still possible to determine if students are assimilating the skills and knowledge they need to be learning without using tests or grades. One way that this can be done is by simply keeping anecdotal, narrative accounts of what a student is achieving as he or she passes through a particular learning progression, and then sharing these with the student as he or she moves through the progression so that the student can see clearly the results of his or her learning. These results are always concrete and personal, not part of some vague, externalized standards that someone else created in order to assess successful learning from their own point of view, rather than from the student's.

# CHAPTER 3

What seems most important in giving young people significant feedback on how well they have learned is that this feedback is somehow intrinsically tied to the learning itself. As students learn a particular subject matter or skill, they receive direct information concerning how they can best proceed with what they are learning; this information is nonjudgmental in nature so that it will not shape the students' views of where they should be directing their attention.

In other words, the evaluation does not cause learners to incorrectly direct their attention away from those aspects of a subject area that might benefit them in order to receive some sort of predetermined adult validation of their learning. In short, the very worst thing that adult evaluations can do is to shape the path of students' learning in a certain direction to the point where the students themselves no longer have any control over it.

Unfortunately, this is exactly what grades and tests do, almost by definition. They shape the paths of young people's learning to the point where the learning itself comes to exist entirely outside of the learner. And yes, admittedly, for students in high school who are applying to colleges, there needs to be a well-documented record of their academic achievements. Yet, what is the point of causing students in their formative years to learn in the sort of disembodied manner that has been alluded to earlier in this chapter?

Once young people grow toward adulthood with a habitual, compulsive need to receive some sort of judgmental, external validation for learning because this has been conditioned into them by their schooling, then those students' education has at last done the sort of permanent damage to them that schools should simply not do to their students. It has taken from them the possibility that their motivation to learn will stem from their curiosities, needs, and interests.

## EVALUATIONS AND DISEMBODIED LEARNING

In our present results-driven culture, unless grades and tests leading toward grades are largely eliminated from our schools for young people in their formative years, we are not dealing with the question of how to make students more effective learners or with how to make their learning more meaningful to them. We're conditioning their learning and personal experience in an unhealthy, neurotic manner.

# 4

# COGNITIVE LEARNING AND STUDENT IMPRESSIONS

It has become an automatic supposition in educating students in their formative years that their learning must be broken up into specific, structured parts, such as one finds in most school curriculums today, so that a particular subject matter can be presented in an organized, effective manner. A large part of this supposition obviously has to do with educators' fears that without highly structured boundaries that serve to focus the learner on the content of what he or she is learning, the learning itself will become haphazard, random, and chaotic. In other words, the fear is that if one doesn't take a certain subject matter and steer it in a specific direction that will acutely focus the student's cognitive understanding of it, then that subject matter will only be explored superficially and chaotically.

For instance, many educators believe that if young people are learning a certain subject matter and are permitted to dwell too long on one particular aspect of it that has made a strong impression upon them, they will not develop a significant grasp of the entire subject area itself. Consequently, it is often assumed that

## CHAPTER 4

the best way for students in their formative years to learn a subject is to keep them focused in a generalized manner on its content, with the large part of this focus having to do with the development of their cognitive faculties.

Probably more than anything, it is this generalized, largely cognitive focus of contemporary schooling that defines what subject matters have come to represent for students in their formative years. Particularly now that scores on standardized tests are becoming the very definition of effective or ineffective learning, this increasingly seems to be the case.

As a result, most schools have adopted into their curriculums the idea that what students learn needs to be presented to them in the form of subject matter that employs a tightly defined, linear approach in order to focus students' attentions. Even with younger children, their learning is increasingly parceled out to them in terms of highly sequential, greatly narrowed areas of learning on which they will be tested.

Certainly, there needs to be a significant amount of cognitive focus in a young person's learning so that he or she can assimilate information in a consistent, orderly fashion. However, once the adult-created agenda of cognition-based subject matter begins to overwhelm the flow of the student's natural interests, then there is a serious danger that both the intensity of the student's curiosities and the richness of his or her impressions will be dissipated to a significant degree.

Any time young people have certain aspects of their environment interrupted before impressions born of their natural interests have come to fruition, the strength of those impressions will tend to grow less vivid. It is only when they are permitted to follow their impressions to a point where they have fully evolved that they will reach their potential power and clarity .

Many times, we needed to pull students at The Children's School away from looking at pictures in books on animal life or evolution, from looking at slides under a microscope, from mixing chemicals at the science table, or from taking apart an old television set in order to return them to lessons for which they had previously agreed to be accountable. And often, later, it seemed regrettable that we had done so. The realization had come, too late, that students were being interrupted just before they were able to fully and impressionistically absorb whatever they were contemplating.

Then, several days later, we would observe that students had little more than a passing interest in what had originally fascinated them a short time earlier because their particular impression had been interrupted before it had come to a point of full fruition. The regretful realization would begin to sink in that certain adult impatience in implementing an agreed-upon lesson, many times with a subject matter that would soon be forgotten, had robbed those young students of an opportunity to comprehend some interesting aspect of their world more fully and directly.

Academic learning, as it exists today in many schools, particularly as a reflection of high-stakes, standardized testing, takes place in such a systematic, preconceived manner that the strength of young people's impressions is continually and significantly diluted by an overemphasis on the development of cognitive skills such as sequential thought, memorization, and classification. Of course, these are skills that are important for students to develop. However, all too often their development comes at the expense of teachers being able to take the time to actually assist their students in how to come more in contact with the strength of their impressions, or else setting up learning environments themselves that can actually facilitate this process.

For example, a class of children is studying plant life as part of their basic biology curriculum. In doing so, the class learns to classify various microscopic life forms into the different categories to which they belong. For instance, algae would be classified as plants because they make food by photosynthesis. On the other hand, protozoa behave like animals and take in food from their environment.

In addition, other microorganisms such as bacteria and viruses are also studied and consequently classified as either plant or animal. In other words, the students are using their newly developed cognitive skills to place different life forms in their appropriate categories. Of course, this is all well and good in that it allows them to better comprehend the subject matter and also permits their developing cognitive structures to become more solidified.

However, if this process becomes too significant too soon, there is also something potentially dangerous taking place: The children may be putting these different microscopic life forms into their different categories, but the classification process might easily begin to overwhelm them with respect to how the different microorganisms are affecting them at an impressionistic level.

We invested money at our school for a decent microscope that we were able to purchase at a great hands-on science education store on the west side of Chicago so that students could use it to look at all sorts of unusual items. Slides of all sorts of tissue from different human organs, all manner of previously dead animals that could be dissected, as well as all sorts of microorganisms—these and many other strange and interesting things found their way to the microscope at The Children's School.

On a good day, particularly one in which all of the teachers had more than their usual reserves of patience, we allowed students to study these things under the microscope until they had had their fill of doing so. If I or one of the other teachers had interrupted the students' fascination with these strange and unusual things by turning them too quickly into a lesson aimed at placing them into categories, we would have in some measure done damage to their evolving inner lives. That is, because the students would have been permitted to go only so far in experiencing the fullness of their impressions, they would have risked accepting the same limited experience in future endeavors.

Of course, there are those who would argue that it is entirely possible for young people to be fully involved in both areas of their life, the impressionistic and the cognitive, at the same time, without the strength of their impressions being at all diluted. However, it is important that those who raise this issue keep in mind that, particularly with children in their formative years, these two areas are much of the time mutually exclusive. Whenever a child must leave intuitive, absorbing experience in order to focus on cognitive skills such as memorization, classification, or any other linear sequence of purely cerebral activities, then his or her primary focus tends to become one of thought processes rather than vivid impressions.

It is very difficult, if not impossible, for children to be equally and fully involved in both types of experience simultaneously. In order for impressions to be experienced to their fullest possible extent, it is imperative that one be able to fully sink into them. If, instead, a child is intently focused on arranging or otherwise systematizing with his or her own thought processes, then the capacity to become fully submerged in his or her impressions is most likely going to be significantly affected.

Of course, a time and place certainly comes for the sorts of mental activities that have to do with cognitive learning. That time and place, however, should come without interfering with any strong impressions that may be germinating within students relative to a particular area of learning, because then the students have been permitted to experience the potential strength of their impressions without having to prematurely leave them before they can grow to their fullest possible fruition.

On the other hand, if young people are compelled to move away from a strong emotive experience before it can grow to

## CHAPTER 4

fruition, then the strength and power of their impressions will only reach a certain level that they may very well not be able to transcend in the future. Once children in their formative years have not experienced certain impressions as fully as they might, then very likely those impressions will be filed away in their memory banks as something that only went so far in terms of how the impressions affected them.

If a student who is fascinated by microorganisms is not permitted to look at these under the microscope or in photographs until the impressions they leave on him or her have reached their fullest possible fruition, the student may well recall how strongly this particular subject matter affected him or her. However, this recollection of emotive experience that only went so far before it was impeded can easily become a self-imposed boundary on how strongly the young person will be able to experience this particular subject area in the future.

When young people are actually able to touch down inside their impressions, at the point where deep truths about some aspects of their world begin to reveal themselves to them beyond the boundaries of systematic thought, they begin to develop a certain pure, clear awareness that often pierces to the core of things.

For instance, the students at The Children's School who were able to intuit the magical, innate geometry that lies at the heart of nature by being provided with the sort of uninterrupted access to microscopic life forms that we gave them were already beginning to develop such awareness. However, if they had come into contact with algae, protozoa, organ tissue, and the like primarily through the processes of categorization or classification, so that they could later be tested on the subject, they would have been moving in an entirely different direction. That is, they would have been moving in the direction of merely manipulating images vis-à-vis their own thought processes.

In the same manner, if a group of older students studying the law and our courts had become acquainted with these things merely through texts and history books on which they would soon be tested, they would not have had a genuine, direct connection with the subject. What we did, however, was to repeatedly take these students to observe civil suits in the courts in downtown Chicago and also to observe criminal trials in the criminal courts just south of the Loop.

Studying in a text how the criminal justice system works and attending malpractice suits and sentencing hearings are two very different realities indeed. The first very soon becomes a pale approximation of the physical reality of our justice system, while the second, of course, "is" that reality. Consequently, without the introduction of the world of courts and trials, there would not have been the same direct connection between these students' emotive life and the real-life particulars of what they were studying. Purely cognitive mental processes are always one step removed from the actual physical realities that lead to the mental images that represent those realities.

Once some aspect of the world that young people inhabit has been turned into a mental image before they have been allowed to fully experience the strength of whatever impression might have been produced, it becomes much more difficult for them to have the same direct contact with the specific area of learning. That is to say, young people will tend to increasingly focus on what is occurring within their own thought processes rather than on how a particular aspect of their world is affecting them. The consequence of this process, over time, is that because young people are able to experience less and less just how strongly different aspects of their world might affect them, they come to accept a significantly dulled version of these.

Eventually, as young people grow toward adulthood, there is an increased chance, because of this particular acceptance of a

# CHAPTER 4

dulled awareness, that they will not be able to experience their world as intensely as they otherwise might. That certainly is a significant price to pay for learning that is often eventually forgotten simply because it is based so largely on cognitive learning on which the students will be tested, rather than through the world of strongly felt experience.

Subject matter, as it exists today in most schools, is so focused on cognitive learning, to the exclusion of impressionistic learning, that it often leaves its students an arm's length away from that which they are studying. Of course, sequential thought and logic, memorization of important facts, and classifying them in order to learn how to generalize are still important skills for all students to develop.

However, assisting young people in how to come more in contact with the strength of their impressions, or else setting up the learning environment itself so that it can actually facilitate this process, are most likely endeavors that few of today's educators, due largely to our current test-oriented culture, would consider to be important or even have time for. Our focus in educating young people has become so results driven and cerebral that we tend to forget that a large part of important learning for students in their formative years needs to be impressionistic and emotive.

Most students, by the time they leave elementary and middle school, or even in many cases high school, will have long forgotten the large number of facts or generalities, many of them irrelevant, with which they have come into contact. However, a young person who has had a specific area of learning, such as the varieties of microscopic life forms or possibly what life was like in a certain historical era, leave a vivid impression on his or her psyche will have gained something that is exceedingly important and permanent. The strength of those feelings will have not only brought the student into contact with underlying levels of truth about certain aspects of his or her immediate environment, but the student's own inner life will have become enriched and energized as well.

Of course, the next question becomes one of how to be certain that young people are acquiring certain knowledge and skills that are important for them to acquire while also facilitating this sort of impressionistic learning. Or, in other words, how might educators develop important cognitive skills and also facilitate the sort of academic learning that will allow students in their formative years to assimilate important subject matter, yet at the same time facilitate the kind of emotive learning alluded to above?

A significant part of the answer to this question surely has to do with finding ways to educate young people so that they can remain with absorbing experiences for as long as they feel inclined to do so, while at the same time facilitating significant academic learning. Particularly this is the case with younger children, in whom the potential strength of their emotive life is still very much an evolving process. Especially with them, it is important that they be permitted to remain with any vivid impressions engendered in them long enough for those impressions to come to full fruition.

For instance, in the case of the students who were interested in looking at different microscopic life forms, and whom we allowed to do so until they had had their fill, the correct time to teach them how to arrange the slides that they were viewing under the microscope into different categories, such as plant or animal, was after they were through looking at them. As long as the cognitive learning did not swallow up the emotive, the strength of the students' impressions was not dulled by the sort of mental activities that might cause them to keep those impressions at arm's length while they focused on the subject matter.

CHAPTER 4

Unfortunately, largely because classroom teachers today know that these sorts of cognitive abilities are entirely the focus of standardized tests, this is exactly the province of most subject matters in today's schools, this diminishment of the student's emotive life through an overemphasis on the cerebral.

In order to change this particular dynamic, our schools need to change so that greater allowances can be made for engrossing, impressionistic experience to occur. However, before that can happen, educators must first begin to rid themselves of at least part of the results-driven mind-set that dominates so much of what they present as subject matter to impressionable young minds.

Then, if the continuity of experience that is important to the individual student is placed squarely in the forefront of educational approaches, the school day can, to a greater extent, be organized around this value, rather than the young person's experience organized around the structure of the school day. Allowances need to be made in the daily schedule for students who wish to continue with learning experiences that are leaving vivid impressions upon them.

In addition, many of the evaluative procedures, such as grading, testing, or the preparation for testing in different subject areas, which often serve only to steer a student in a specific, limited direction, need to be greatly reduced. Consequently, there will be more time in the school day for students to stay with experiences that naturally absorb them.

Just as importantly, teaching approaches can be applied that address both the emotive and cognitive aspects of young people's learning. For instance, teaching various sciences in a manner that allows students to impressionistically experience that with which they are coming into contact, rather than relying too heavily on the memorization of facts and information on which they can be tested, would be a necessary step.

## COGNITIVE LEARNING AND STUDENT IMPRESSIONS

Granted, young people's cognitive development is extremely important; facilitating that in ways that permit them to become more logical, more introspective, and more aware of the world of ideas has an obviously significant place in our schools. Certainly these need to take place if students are ever going to reach their full potential. However, educators need to also keep in mind that as most young people grow toward adulthood and leave their schooling behind, the part of that education that is often most significant to them is that which contains the richness and intensity of strong impressions accrued from what they have learned.

To continually overemphasize cognition-based learning to the point where the impressions of students in their formative years that were once undiluted, powerful, and clear are significantly dulled is to engender the development of human beings who lose much of their original capacity to vividly experience the world that they inhabit. Again, educating young minds to think clearly and to properly organize their thought processes in relation to what they are learning is, of course, an essential endeavor. However, a way needs to be found to do so while, at the same time, leaving the vitality of young people's impressions intact.

Many people live their lives with their own responses to the world in which they find themselves significantly dulled, and at least one significant reason for this is not so very hard to discover. It has to do with the manner in which they were educated as young people, when they were often not permitted to take their experience to a point of completion. As a result, this has set in motion a pattern in their lives in which their experience of their world remains significantly dulled and diluted, a pattern that they have come to eventually accept.

Acquiring facts, information, and skills is only part of what makes a successful learner. In addition, developing the capacity

## CHAPTER 4

to become truly submerged in the potential intensity of impressions engendered in one by a particular area of learning is just as important and needs to be treated as such by teachers of students in their formative years. However, for this to occur, we need to begin by realizing that fostering vivid, impressionistic experience in young people is more important than the current high-stakes, standardized testing programs that in many schools threaten to entirely overwhelm such experience.

# 5

# ADULT PRECONCEPTIONS AND STUDENT NEEDS

How schools go about meeting the needs of their students is, of course, a fundamental concern. More specifically, how does the approach that a particular school employs address the needs of its individual students so that the school's philosophy and students' needs don't come to resemble two parallel lines that are never meant to intersect? In such a circumstance, the school's philosophy keeps being retooled and reshaped by those who administer the school, without any assurance that it is truly connecting with the needs of the young people in the school. The experience of the students continues to be whatever it is, disconnected from the evolution of the school's methodology.

Of course, many educators tend to believe that young people's needs cannot be met if there is not some sort of organized, philosophical underpinning that will allow their behavior to be seen within a certain context. Such educators also probably believe that without a predetermined approach in place, students' lives and learning will inevitably proceed in a chaotic, haphazard manner. In other words, they are convinced that a well-conceived

# CHAPTER 5

philosophy is the only way to guarantee that student needs are met, rather than allowing the philosophy to originate with these needs themselves.

However, considering this view of educational approaches and student needs, it would seem that one has to indeed ask if this is putting the cart squarely in front of the horse. If the approach that a specific school employs with its students doesn't germinate directly from their individual needs, then what is the real point of this approach? That is, if the approach employed with the students in the school is predetermined prior to the students coming to school at the beginning of the school year, then how can one possibly be certain that this preconceived methodology is meeting their actual needs?

Many educators will give the obvious answer that because childhood development and learning have been studied so thoroughly, it is indeed possible to speculate on how one might foster both healthy development and meaningful learning by developing intelligent approaches based on what we already know. Then, because one has conceived philosophies and methodologies based on what educators have already discovered about how young people best learn and grow in a healthy manner, those who administer the philosophy or methodology in a particular school can be reasonably certain that they are meeting the needs of their students.

However, in considering this issue, one still has to ask if it actually makes sense to adopt a specific approach to educating students in a certain milieu before one has even gotten to know them as individuals. In asking this question, one has to go even further and ask the more probing question of what happens if the needs of specific students in a school are not best served by the prevailing methodology. In point of fact, one has to ask what teachers will do in the case of students whose needs are not met by the school's particular approach. Will teachers and administrators then throw out their preconceived approach in order to meet their specific needs?

Naturally, many educators will reply to these questions by simply saying that it is possible for teachers and schools, even though their particular approaches to learning may be predetermined, to be flexible enough to still meet student needs. For example, they might argue that even though a teacher in a particular classroom is operating according to the prevailing approach employed by the school in educating its students, the teacher can still employ methods and approaches with his or her students that will meet what the teacher observes to be their individual needs. And in the context of the classroom setting, at least to a certain extent, this is indeed true. The teacher will be able to both instruct and relate to different students differently based on what he or she perceives to be their unique needs.

However, if the approach that teachers employ in their classrooms is preconceived prior to the beginning of the school year, increasingly because it is expected of teachers that their students will produce certain results on standardized tests, then the learning environment that the teachers create will inevitably evolve from those preconceptions. Consequently, responses to their students will often be limited by the very environment that the teachers themselves have created. That is, because teachers must function within the confines of a predetermined structure that has evolved from certain expectations of the empirical results their students will produce, teachers' responses to their students will be limited by that very structure.

In addition, because teachers are increasingly viewing the students in their classrooms through the prism of these standardized test results, it becomes very easy for them to fall into the trap of viewing the behavior and learning of their students only through that particular prism. They begin making assumptions about the needs of the individual students in their classroom according to

CHAPTER 5

where the young person's behavior and learning style fit into a preconceived approach that is based largely on attaining certain empirical results.

For example, a student who has had unpredictable, inconsistent responses from the adults in his life attends a typical contemporary school in which the curriculum is very structured and very results oriented. Therefore, because his teacher feels it is important to adhere strictly to a preplanned curriculum that prepares children for success on certain standardized tests, she becomes insistent that her students approach their learning in a certain manner so that they can absorb the curriculum.

However, this particular student, because of past inconsistent responses from adults that he has had to endure, often needs the sort of clarity that comes from knowing exactly why he has to learn a subject in a certain manner. So, because in this particular environment there really isn't time for this, he may well begin to disengage himself from a learning situation that doesn't make sense to him.

Then, because of his potential inattentiveness, he might very likely come to be seen as someone who is unmotivated or who is not interested in learning, when this may not be true at all. He may be potentially interested in many different subject areas and even highly motivated. However, he just begins to mentally drift away when there isn't a well-defined pattern of consistent adult responses that define his learning for him.

So, because he may most likely be seen as an unmotivated and uninterested learner, his primary need now is seen to be the development of the motivation to learn. Consequently, this false perception of his real needs can then set in motion a whole pattern of adult responses to him that are not only not necessary but that also give him a false message about himself. Over time, this false message begins to turn into a self-fulfilling prophecy as his teacher continues to respond to him as someone who is unmotivated and uninterested in any particular subject matter.

A couple of the students who came to The Children's School were two extremely bright nine- and ten-year-old boys. One of them had been homeschooled, while the other had attended another alternative school. Both of them were also extremely shy. In fact, it took both of them several months after they arrived at the school to open up and talk much with anyone, either students or teachers.

In retrospect, it would have been very easy for teachers in a more traditional school who must significantly narrow their focus in order to prepare their students for success on certain standardized tests to confuse the shyness of both of these students with a genuine withdrawal from the objects of their learning—probably because the teachers wouldn't be able to observe the students more clearly simply because there wouldn't be enough time to do so without putting the performance level of the other students in the classroom at risk.

Consequently, both of these students, who were exceptionally bright and talented, might well have had their shyness confused with a lack of interest in the particular subject matter they were studying if they had been in a more results-driven setting. Then, as their teacher responded to them accordingly, their potential further interest in the objects of their learning might have indeed been compromised by their teacher's increased lack of involvement with them when he or she mistakenly assumed the boys' lack of interest. Predetermined, results-driven approaches to learning will simply not meet the needs of a number of students in any learning environment when individual needs do not match those of a particular school's methodology. In addition, these preconceived approaches often lead toward incorrect perceptions of all those young people whose genuine needs as learners do not fit the preconceived approach.

# CHAPTER 5

Unfortunately, this pattern is transpiring in many of today's schools, and there is really only one way to avoid it. To be sure that a particular school is able to take into account the different potential needs of the students in it, the school must have no predetermined approach rigidly in place prior to the beginning of the school year.

We accomplished this, eventually, by beginning each school year by sitting down with students individually, with their parents also in attendance, and developing lesson plans. For the first four or five years that the school was in existence, we adhered to an abbreviated version of this, in which we listed all the students' interests in any number of different areas on a large piece of poster board (from the very familiar, such as prehistoric reptiles, to the more idiosyncratic, such as Irish folk dancing) and then developed individual plans with students pertaining to their basic skills.

However, as our little school grew, it became increasingly obvious that each student needed a highly specific learning plan in order to focus his or her attention. An approach was developed in which the philosophy of the school, if one can call it that, lay entirely within the plans that were developed for each individual student. That is, there was no predetermined approach to any given school year other than these individual plans.

In addition, it became apparent over time that because any number of different levels of motivation, cooperation, and cognitive ability entered the school each year, how a lesson plan was hammered out and implemented with a particular student had to factor in these sorts of differences. Therefore, the approach of the school could really only be described in terms of how we tried to meet the needs of each individual student, both academically and personally. There really was no other philosophy or methodology.

There is no other way to view the different possible approaches to which any student in a particular school might be exposed on the way to meeting his or her individual needs than to operate without any sort of generalized methodology. As long as there is some sort of adult-conceived methodology inflexibly in place, the students in the school will be inherently viewed in terms of how they react to the particular methodology and not in terms of how they might react to different approaches that might be tried with them until their genuine needs are met.

Of course, related to this question of needs that are merely symptoms and those that are causes is the issue of how needs in young people might evolve in a manner that is part of an overall healthy personal development—that is, one in which the young person is making increasing contact with the world through his or her direct experience of it, rather than evolving in a manner in which certain needs are conditioned into young people before their actual experience of their learning environment has had a chance to come to full fruition.

If the needs of a student are merely symptoms but are identified primarily as causes, then it becomes very easy for a pattern to be set in motion between teacher and student in which false needs are created in the learner. Most of the time, this occurs when a teacher develops a false image of the young person due to the teacher's confusion of symptoms with causes, and then relates to the student accordingly.

For instance, the teacher of a student in his formative years who wants to learn on his own so that he can digest information and knowledge in a more holistic fashion, rather than as part of a rigidly preconceived step-by-step progression, might easily come to view this particular student as easily distracted or inattentive. This might occur when the student, who is asked to learn the step-by-step curriculum as part of a group of other students, begins to disengage himself from the lessons so that he can try to piece together their contents in a more holistic fashion. Then, as a result of this, it becomes increasingly easy for his teacher to

## CHAPTER 5

confuse this disengagement with a mind that is easily distracted or inattentive.

In doing so, his teacher might then begin to relate to the student as someone who is in fact distractible or unable to focus, rather than as simply someone who needs more personal space in learning situations in order to get his mind around specific knowledge or information as part of a whole before focusing more closely on it. Then, because young people tend to actually become the messages that they are given about themselves, and also because this pattern of relating to the student as someone who is inattentive might easily be picked up by many of the other students in the learning environment, the student might well begin to have difficulties focusing on his learning.

This particular dynamic might easily occur when the student is put in the untenable position of having to relate to others as the person that he is not. That is, if his teacher begins to speak and relate to him during group lessons as she would to someone who can't really focus on relevant subject matter, and the other students begin to do the very same thing, the student can very easily become caught in this particular pattern of relations with others. Eventually, as this pattern becomes more and more established, the student might well start to become easily distracted and inattentive.

This will tend to occur as his teacher, and also possibly some of the other students in the class, try to compel him to focus more on the particulars of the knowledge and information on which they know they will be tested rather than on absorbing the subject matter as a whole. Then, as he attempts to learn in a manner that is not best suited to his optimal learning style, he might indeed become easily distracted as he attempts to focus on isolated bits of information as part of a group of students who are all following the same learning progression.

## ADULT PRECONCEPTIONS AND STUDENT NEEDS

Because the students at The Children's School learned on a highly individualized basis instead of as part of a group of students all learning the same thing simultaneously, it was possible to observe many of the subtleties of their different personalities, motivations, and learning styles, and so it tended to become easier to distinguish causes from symptoms.

One student resisted learning mathematics not because she was afraid of the subject or didn't have a facility for it but because she felt pressure from her parents to do so, and so engaged in this sort of nonlearning as a means of holding onto her dignity. Another student had a strong need to secretly compete with a slightly older student in progressing with her work. So when he began to lose interest in a subject, so did she. Still another extremely bright older student would regularly spurn attempts by teachers to teach him to write more coherent sentences and to work on his spelling with him, not because he didn't think he needed to do so, but because he operated at such a high level in everything else, his writing and spelling skills had become a source of embarrassment to him.

All of these reactions to learning in certain areas, which were genuine causes, could have been very easily turned into false needs in other classrooms where learning was not so individualized. The student who refused to learn math in opposition to her parents' wishes could have been confused with someone who didn't want to learn mathematics simply because she doubted her ability to do so.

The student who lost a certain amount of interest in learning a certain subject when the boy with whom she was competitive began to lose interest could have been seen as someone who had hit a certain cognitive plateau that she simply wasn't able to get past. And the older student who didn't want to accept help with his spelling and writing due to a certain amount of embarrassment

CHAPTER 5

might well have been labeled as simply lazy in another, more results-driven learning environment.

Any rigidly preconceived philosophy or methodology employed with young people in a particular school in order to achieve certain quantifiable results is going to be inherently based on suppositions about the needs of the school's individual students as learners. In fact, in our present educational climate, that's what preconceived approaches to the education of students in their formative years are all about, this idea that the adults who create the approach necessarily know in advance what students need in order to best empirically demonstrate their learning. Consequently, because young people in today's schools are often viewed by those who teach them according to how well they perform on specific high-stakes standardized tests, those young people are inevitably going to have to respond to their teacher in terms of the learner they are being seen as.

So those students whose ability to learn exceeds what their test scores would indicate are now often put in the position of having to relate to their teachers by either acquiescing to this perception of their abilities as being inferior and then allowing themselves to be taught according to this false perception or else reacting against the way they are being taught.

As a result of this, both groups might begin to develop false needs. If it's the case of students who simply accept the preconceived manner in which they are being seen, those false needs will evolve simply because they have acquiesced to being someone whom they are not in order to learn. Yet, if the students react to an approach that doesn't seem right for them because they sense that it underestimates their abilities, then their needs will often evolve from this pattern of reaction, rather than from what their genuine needs were before they came to the learning situation.

These things will tend to occur largely because, again, young people so often tend to become the very messages that they are given about themselves. That is, students whose scores on a certain standardized test for a particular subject matter place them at a certain level in their classroom at school, and who are then taught according to that particular level, will begin to see themselves as having capacities only at that level, even though this might not actually be the case. They may, for example, have a much greater facility for learning the particular subject matter or skill but just doesn't test well.

Then, because of test scores, if student are taught as learners who have only a certain capacity in absorbing the particular learning area, they will tend to increasingly see themselves in this same, limited manner. Consequently, they will begin to expect less of themselves and actually set limits upon themselves concerning what they are able to achieve. As a result, they now possess certain needs relative to a certain subject area that they might never have had if they were not being perceived according to their test results.

On the other hand, if their test results place them at a level that they instinctively sense they can in fact transcend and they are still being taught according to their low test scores, then they may well react to being taught in this manner by becoming undisciplined and inattentive in order not to acquiesce to an approach to learning that they sense inherently puts limits on them. In order to begin to learn according to their potential, they will, given the limited parameters of the learning environment in which they find themselves, actually need to become more disciplined and attentive, even though neither of these was an original need of theirs.

What is often so damaging about the evolution of these sorts of false needs in young people isn't just that it sets in motion a pattern of relating to others as someone whom they are not, but that it also prevents them from fully connecting with both subject matter and the learning environment itself. To genuinely connect

CHAPTER 5

with a specific subject, or the learning environment in which they find themselves, students must do so as the persons, or learners, that they really are.

Needless to say, feeling perpetually at arm's length from whatever one is endeavoring to learn, and from the learning environment itself, has repercussions that can easily extend far into the young person's future. For one thing, quite obviously, students not only learn less quickly, but they also begin to doubt their ability to learn, particularly when they see other students accessing information, knowledge, and skills more quickly than they are able to do. However, just as significantly, their curiosities, their will to achieve, and even the strength of their impressions may well be markedly diluted when they are not able to become fully absorbed in the objects of their learning.

Predetermined approaches to young people's learning that are based on the need by educators to produce certain empirical results often lead to incorrect perceptions of students whose genuine needs do not fit either the preconceived approach or their own test results. These incorrect perceptions then often lead toward the evolution of false needs when students' teachers confuse reactions of these students with needs of theirs that are genuine. In so doing, teachers tend to create learning situations that compel students to respond to them in a false manner. This inauthentic manner of responding to one's learning environment frequently leads toward students' lack of connection with it, and thus to experience that is incomplete.

In order to change this damaging pattern of development in young people, which is prevalent in many of our schools today, it is necessary that teachers be able to teach in environments that permit them to clearly perceive the needs of their individual students and then to develop methods and curricula out of those same perceptions, rather than having to adapt themselves and their students to preconceived approaches that originate largely with the desire to produce certain standardized test scores.

This was where the process of democratic negotiation with students became a real boon to our efforts at The Children's School. We were often able to work our way through certain issues with students in a way in which we wouldn't have been able to if we had been forced to implement a rigidly preconceived philosophy.

For example, we had several students raised by parents who gave their children a great deal of latitude but also insisted that when they made mistakes, they suffer the consequences of their actions. As a result of this, nearly all of these students, some of them still quite young, were able to adopt a real no-nonsense approach to their learning. They needed to know the exact reasons why it was important for them to learn something, and if they felt that those reasons were too vague, they grew more insistent. This particular stance of theirs would often concern some of the basic skills, such as mathematics, spelling, or basic geography, that they, initially at least, saw no point in learning.

Especially in a democratic school that attempts to give students a genuine voice in their learning, telling these students that they needed to learn these sorts of skills simply because "you need them" would have been one step away from genuine heresy. In working our way through this particular issue with these students, the teachers in the school were able to get in touch with their individual needs in ways that we possibly couldn't if we hadn't begun our process of negotiation.

Out of this process of negotiating individually with the different students, we were able to hammer out approaches that stemmed from the needs of each. One older boy, who was extremely creative, was allowed to stretch out his learning of mathematics over a week so that he could take time to focus each day on the art that was so important to him. Another older girl, who was very ambitious and competitive, was willing to work on her

## CHAPTER 5

spelling if she could also learn calculus. Another younger boy, who wanted to feel on par with the older boys in the school, was willing to work harder on his basic math skills if I would agree to also teach him geometry a couple of times each week.

In point of fact, there really is only one way to be certain that the approach to learning that one is employing with a particular student is meeting his or her needs as a learner, and that is to actually create the approach out of the clear, unbiased, day-to-day observation of the student in the specific environment in which he or she exists. Otherwise, the philosophy and approach of a particular school are indeed like two parallel lines that never intersect. The philosophy continues to evolve from adult ideas concerning what will produce the best empirical validations of significant learning while the experience of the students continues to be whatever it is, significantly unrelated to these presuppositions.

However, there is indeed a way for educational philosophy and student experience to actually intersect, and that is for the approach that one employs with young people to actually germinate from their individual needs, with the possibility always existing that one might change course whenever it is deemed important enough to do so.

This means, of course, not only a significant examination of the entire results-driven culture that contemporary education has now produced but also a much greater individualizing of young people's education. This is necessary so that the approaches that are used with different students evolve directly from their individual needs and learning styles, rather than compelling them to sublimate those needs and learning styles to approaches to learning that educators hope will best produce certain empirical results.

As much as anything, it is this individualizing of students' education that is the most important ingredient for positive change in our schools, more important than all the controls that are presently in place to compel young people to acquire specific knowledge and skills according to predetermined timetables. It is also more important than particular results on high-stakes standardized tests that give both students and educators such a false message that it is only the endpoint, and not the journey, that is important in the learning process.

# 6

# DEVELOPMENTAL CONCERNS

Our schools have always been institutions that are equated first and foremost with academic learning. That is to say, a successful school is, most of the time, seen as one in which the students who attend it achieve certain academic goals. Of course, it's also been important that young people are developmentally healthy and that they develop such attributes as self-confidence and the capacity to relate to others. However, the most important component of schools and education has nearly always been academic learning. Of course, for the most part, this primary emphasis on academics seems entirely appropriate. Such learning is obviously something that often leads toward future success in life.

However, granted that academic learning should always have an essential, primary place in young people's education, there is still the question of what place developmental concerns should play in the entire learning process. Should these be addressed during the course of a student's schooling as issues that, although highly important, need to be dealt with apart from academic learning? Or should these developmental concerns actually become part and parcel of a young person's academic progress? Or, furthermore, does successful academic learning necessarily imply that the learning is in fact built first on a healthy developmental base?

If a young person is having difficulties with his or her academic learning, is it primarily an academic problem, or do certain developmental needs have to be met before the student can become successful with his or her academics? In other words, are there other aspects of a student's life in school that should not only come before academic learning but indeed should become the very basis on which such learning is built?

For example, if younger students are having difficulty learning to read, is it primarily an academic problem or is it because they lack self-confidence around their peers because they were never given enough room to explore, and feel comfortable in, their school environment when they were first making the separation from their parents? Or if older students are uninterested in academic learning, if nothing seems to grab them, is this primarily a matter of getting the correct subject matter in front of them, or is it because they were not given enough time to pursue the successful peer relations that they so desperately crave? Consequently, everything else pales next to that particular vital concern of theirs.

If the answers to these questions lie, first and foremost, in the sorts of developmental issues that have just been raised, then it would seem to make sense for educators to attempt to ascertain how they might more effectively make these concerns an integral part of young people's learning. If we continue to isolate academic learning and personal, developmental issues from each other, as is done in so many classrooms today, neither students' academic learning nor their personal development will be built on a solid base.

## DEVELOPMENTAL CONCERNS

For instance, it may indeed be the case that the capacity to form successful relationships with peers is something that needs, by its very nature, to occur before a young person is able to become wholeheartedly absorbed in interests that lead toward academic skills. If this is indeed the case, it would seem to make sense for teachers to make allowances during the school day for students in their formative years to develop this capacity to form meaningful relationships with peers, even if it means that occasionally they will not focus so intently on purely academic concerns.

Likewise, it may be true that a younger student needs to initially establish a feeling of personal independence in his or her learning environment before becoming fully engaged by group activities with other children. If this were indeed the case, then it would be important to allow that student to roam and explore the classroom in order to feel more secure before he or she becomes more involved with group learning activities.

In other words, there may indeed be an inherent, natural progression of developmental and academic concerns that students in their formative years must traverse so that their personal development and learning evolve on a firm base. Then, if this were indeed the case, it seems logical to suggest that it is important for students to attain certain capacities during each stage of the progression so that they are able to fully ground themselves at that particular stage.

In addition, this would seem to be true even if that stage has primarily to do with personal concerns rather than purely academic ones. If a young person has not first attained the needed capacities at a certain stage of personal development, it tends to become much more difficult for him or her to become fully grounded in learning.

For example, students who haven't been able to form meaningful relationships with their peers will often have their ability

CHAPTER 6

to attend to academic learning compromised when their attention is continually being diverted as they try to make themselves more secure around other students. In the same manner, if younger children aren't given adequate time to explore their school environment as a means of becoming more independent and secure, it will be much harder for them to focus their attention on group lessons when other children are around with whom they haven't yet established this security.

What tends to make this all true is the simple fact that, if allowed to do so, a young person will inevitably gravitate in the direction of his or her most important developmental need. If, at a particular point in development, a child's most important need is to establish independence and to begin the process of separation from his or her parents, then that child will become easily engaged by those aspects of his or her environment that allow this. Very likely, the child might be found moving toward the periphery of a group of children around whom he or she feels comfortable in order to become increasingly part of the school environment, rather than remain alone and inwardly focused on home.

Likewise, if another student's more important developmental need is to develop the capacity to relate to peers, then he or she will almost certainly seek out another student with whom some sort of meaningful relationship can be formed. This desire to do so will, most of the time, be far more important to the student than success at attaining any particular academic skill, and consequently, the teacher should give this desire its proper due when dealing with this particular student. In this regard, the student should have his or her genuine attempts to relate to a member of the peer group significantly factored into any schedule that the school or classroom has adopted for academic learning.

These two issues, independence and peer relations in relation to academic learning, were things we came into contact with on a consistent basis at The Children's School. Especially in regard to younger children, we often found ourselves dealing with students who had temporarily abandoned their academic work in order to either make themselves more comfortable in the classroom by observing what others were doing, or else attempting to become friendly with another student with whom they wished to develop some sort of relationship.

In both cases, we had to invariably weigh the student's academic progress and inner discipline against the possibility that the student was in an actual position to be successful at meeting an important developmental need. And we invariably found, when looking back retrospectively at the end of the school day, that when we returned a student to academics who was either taking time to closely observe the learning of others or else genuinely trying to relate to a peer, that our decision had indeed been a mistake. Later on when they occurred, these sorts of developmental breakthroughs were often the very key to significant academic progress in these same students.

If there is in fact a certain inherent sequence of developmental and academic stages that will naturally occur in a young person's life if it is permitted to do so, then it is surely our job as educators to determine the order in which certain aspects of this sequence become important. If we were able to do that, then we would have a much better idea than we do now of exactly what activities, either academic or interpersonal, it is important for a student in his or her formative years to engage in at any particular point in life. In addition, we would also possess a better idea of how to assist young people, particularly younger children, in becoming secure at the specific stage in the progression that they currently inhabit.

This doesn't necessarily mean, by any stretch of the imagination, that students shouldn't become engaged in academics until they are relating well to peers, or that younger children won't significantly pursue their curiosities until they have established greater independence from home. What is meant here is that if students in their formative years haven't become secure and fulfilled at a particular stage in this naturally evolving sequence, then the subsequent stages will evolve on a weak base. A good analogy for this would be a pyramid that is weakly constructed because those blocks at the levels below or preceding the top levels are not firmly in place.

Consequently, those stages at the top of the hypothetical pyramid, which would of course tend to concern academic more than developmental issues, will not be securely part of the young person's development simply because there is always the chance that a stage below them will adversely affect them. For example, students who have never really become secure in relating to peers are perpetually in danger of having their academic focus interrupted by the behavior of other students. Likewise, children who have not yet separated from their parents in a manner that allows them to come to school as fully independent people will be consistently one step away from being able to immerse themselves in their interests simply because they have never fully arrived in their learning environment.

Therefore, if one wishes to provide a learning environment for young people in which their personal growth is being optimally fostered and in which they are able to fully focus on their academic learning, then it seems imperative that the requisite developmental stages upon which such learning needs to be built are allowed to evolve to their fullest possible extent. In other words, it would be vitally important that students in their formative years be permitted to fully engage themselves with any concern that addresses important developmental needs.

In addition, it would be necessary that they actually be assisted by their teachers in doing so. Otherwise, there are going to be incomplete areas or gaps in their personal development. Conse-

DEVELOPMENTAL CONCERNS

quently, their learning will not be as focused or as significant to them as it might potentially be.

What this means, of course, is that educators of students in their formative years, particularly of younger children, must give more attention to personal, developmental issues than is now the case. Indeed, it would even appear to be true that they should work to foster healthy developmental growth as an actual precondition for fully focused, meaningful academic learning. It is this, as much as anything, that will allow students' learning to be built on the sort of solid base that will permit young people to become absorbed in it because they have already become secure at those developmental stages upon which such learning tends to be built.

However, if educators are going to ascertain if there is in fact a certain natural progression of developmental and academic concerns for students in their formative years, or if teachers are going to be given the latitude to better assist their students with the sorts of developmental issues on which their academic learning most likely needs to be grounded, then the basic approach of many of our schools must change.

Unfortunately what is happening is that rigidly conceived approaches, curricula, and methodologies are being increasingly introduced to ensure optimal results on certain standardized tests. As a result of this, not only is there very little time left over for dealing with the sorts of developmental concerns alluded to above, but the actual structure of our results-oriented classrooms tends to work entirely against this occurring.

For instance, a student who needs to spend more time attempting to relate to other students is consistently pulled away from doing so by her teacher so that she can attend to predetermined, compulsory lessons concerning subject matter on which she will be tested. So it becomes significantly harder for her to find something that truly interests her when she is preoccupied

CHAPTER 6

with sharpening relational skills that she is not being given enough time to sharpen.

Likewise, another student who is developing his confidence by engaging in self-created art is not given enough time to do so because of his school's rigid daily schedule, which has evolved in large measure from fears that students will not be adequately prepared to perform well on particular standardized tests. Consequently, he is unable to gain the confidence he needs in order to attempt more significant relations with peers.

The only way to be certain that these students will have their needs met in a manner that allows them to proceed in a healthy fashion from one developmental/learning issue to another is to simply dispense with the sort of rigidity that now permeates so many of our classrooms due to the current fear and obsession over students not performing well on certain high-stakes standardized tests. Then it will be possible to give students the latitude that they need to seek out and fulfill themselves at whatever developmental/learning stage most requires their attention. In addition, their teachers will be more able to take the time to provide them with the kind of attention and direction that they need in order to do this.

Students who need to have enough time to learn through their observations and experience how to relate to different peers differently will have sufficient time each day to do just that. Their teachers will have the time to provide them with suggestions and direction that will help them become successful in their efforts to relate. Teachers and students will have these opportunities because they will no longer be tied to inflexible daily structures that don't permit them to take time for this kind of teaching and learning.

Likewise, students who need enough time each day to become more self-confident through their art, for example, and then to use that increased confidence when dealing with peers, will be given time to do this when the rigid scheduling of the school day no longer prevents them from fully expressing themselves through their artistic proclivities.

Consequently, because the correct developmental/learning sequence is permitted to occur naturally, young people will be able to experience genuine successes at the particular stage that they eventually inhabit. They will be successes born of having been allowed to fully devote their attention to personal and academic issues toward which they are instinctively gravitating. When they move to the next inherent developmental or learning stage that is now significant to them, they will be able to do so without the previous stage still demanding their attention

When students who need the latitude to seek out and learn how to appropriately relate to peers have been truly able to do so, they will tend to become more easily absorbed in their learning and interests. They will most likely not continue to be distracted by the actions of those around them to whom they are not yet successfully relating. And when the students who need time each day to develop their self-confidence through their creativity are allowed to do just that, and are even assisted in doing so, they have a much better chance of relating well to peers because of their increased confidence in themselves.

If one indeed wishes to provide a learning environment for young people in which their personal growth is being optimally fostered and in which they are able to fully focus on their learning, then it seems imperative that the requisite developmental stages upon which such learning is often based be allowed to evolve to their fullest possible extent. In other words, it is vitally important that students in their formative years in any learning environment be permitted to fully engage themselves at any stage that addresses significant developmental needs.

In addition, it is necessary that they actually be assisted by their teachers in this process. Otherwise, there are going to be incomplete areas or gaps in their personal development. As a result, their learning is very likely not going to be as focused or significant to them as it might potentially be.

Therefore, facilitating this sort of complete involvement in young people's lives and learning should be a primary concern of all educators. Without it, we are merely training students in various academic and social skills and not allowing them to make these skills their own by virtue of being permitted to become fully involved in their development.

It is possible to provide this more developmentally based approach and to still have orderly, sequential, significant learning occur in students who benefit from it. The key is creating the time and space in our schools that will allow young people, particularly younger children, to become well grounded in the earlier stages of the above progression—independence, self-confidence, and developing successful relations with peers.

If these things occur, it will be much easier for students to become fully engaged in developing and pursuing meaningful interests and in giving themselves more fully to the pursuit of those academic skills that they need to acquire. They will be able to do so because they have already had their important developmental needs met.

Of course, because there weren't the sorts of external controls at The Children's School on student behavior and learning that there are in more traditional schools—constriction of free movement during the course of the school day, poor grades to be explained to parents, the standard trip to the principal's office—the developmental issues previously mentioned tended to affect academic learning at our school much more directly.

Younger students who came to us before they had established a healthy independence from their parents couldn't be compelled to become involved in their academic learning in the way that they might be compelled elsewhere. Students who were afraid of challenges because their parents had either done too much for them or else simply overprotected them couldn't be required to address certain abilities, such as learning to read, before they felt themselves to be ready.

Students who hadn't been able to establish meaningful relationships with their peers were often distracted from their academic work by the activities of other students within the classroom setting. And because the students in our school were given relative freedom of movement throughout the school day, this sort of distraction couldn't be so easily controlled.

In observing this, those of us who taught at the school really were in a unique position to see the very direct effects of developmental issues upon academic learning. As a result of this, our responses to academic concerns often originated with a much greater developmental focus than that which is most likely employed in many other schools; issues of independence, self-confidence, and peer relations became rapidly a part of learning to read, write, and work with numbers.

However, in looking back at what occurred at our school over the years, we probably could have been more intrusive than we were in confronting certain parents with how they were raising their children. In an open, democratic learning environment such as ours, parents who are overprotective, spoil their children, or don't set clear limits with them can unwittingly engender any number of difficulties with their academic learning. At that point, there is no question about it. Educators have an actual responsibility to be very direct with parents in regard to developmental issues.

Far too often, our schools place academic learning and personal development in separate boxes, so to speak, and in so doing often cause the former to be experienced by students in their formative years as an impediment that keeps them from becoming more involved with the latter. This occurs when young people's

CHAPTER 6

interpersonal and other developmental concerns are put aside because they are thought to be less important than academics, and in the bargain, young people often feel that they are not being allowed to address these personal issues as fully as they might. Consequently, they often give up trying to do so, which unfortunately tends to become a pattern in their lives, regardless of whether they are in or out of school.

Needless to say, relegating a young person's developmental concerns to a secondary place of importance (i.e., something to be taken care of after school or during recess) does not allow for his or her full development as a person. Because students are so often given the message these days that their personal concerns are secondary to their academic curriculum, their daily schedule, their grades, or their performance on particular standardized tests, personal concerns frequently become, over time, secondary to them. As a result of this, they don't end up focusing on them as fully as they otherwise might.

Teachers in today's classrooms should be given greater latitude to temporarily set aside academic learning, as well as any preexisting educational structures, in order to allow students the requisite time and space they need to become fully engaged by significant developmental concerns. In addition, students should be consistently assisted by adults in developing strategies for success with these concerns. Consequently, educators would most likely find that they are actually fostering environments in which young people's learning is becoming more grounded, and also more significant to them, because it has been permitted to evolve on a more solid base.

Yet none of this can occur if we don't find ways to assess student learning other than the "test scores and grades are everything" mentality that now permeates many of our schools. Once empirical results become synonymous with success, something that has almost become a fully institutionalized process, then the important developmental concerns on which meaningful learning tends to be built go rapidly out the window. A results-driven mind-set on the part of educators will nearly always lead toward standardized approaches to learning aimed at producing the sorts of results in students that inevitably ignore the unique journey on which any learner needs to be allowed to embark in comprehending various subject matters.

In addition, once a significant part of young people's school days is taken up with results-driven curricula that attempt to engender higher test scores in highly specific areas or with preparing students for, or actually administering, certain standardized tests, there is going to be little time left over for assisting them with the significant developmental or interpersonal issues on which their academic learning often needs to be based.

Therefore, a choice has to be made. Does one want attention given to producing higher test scores or does one want more meaningful, fully grounded learning? The two are indeed often mutually exclusive entities simply by virtue of the fact that once one starts to steer personal experience and learning in young people in a certain direction in an attempt to achieve certain external results, then one becomes less concerned with what is transpiring inside the student as he or she learns, because one is then predominately concerned only with the results that that learning produces.

# 7

# A JUST EQUILIBRIUM

The vast majority of educational environments for young people, even those employing more open-ended concepts, tend to evolve with the teachers in them functioning as figures of authority in relation to the students. That is to say, the adults are in charge of setting up the environment in advance of the young people arriving in it, and of making sure that it operates in the manner in which they intend it to operate. In other words, if a particular classroom is not meeting the needs of the students, if those students are not learning, or if the students and the teacher are not genuinely connecting, then it becomes the job of the teacher and other educators in the school to fix the situation.

This has been the essential approach to dealing with problems that are developing within a particular learning environment for about as long as any of us can remember. If young people are not learning or if their individual needs aren't being met, then it is up to the teachers to either change their basic approach or else try to restructure the environment itself in order to more effectively address these two difficulties. If the teacher and students don't

CHAPTER 7

seem to be genuinely connecting, then it is up to the teacher to somehow change the personal dynamics in the classroom so that this can occur.

Of course, all of this appears at first glance to be so patently obvious that many educators would tend to wonder why one even brings the matter up at all. Naturally, if there are difficulties occurring in a particular learning environment, it is the responsibility of the adult to address and correct the problems through careful consideration. After all, the students in a specific classroom are in the classroom teacher's charge; if there are difficulties, the teacher is the professional who should have the expertise to address them.

Even in most educational environments that are said to be essentially student centered, this is still the basic approach that is employed whenever difficulties arise. However, in many of these environments, as opposed to more traditional ones, the idea is to change the actual learning environment in some manner so that students are better able to adapt themselves to it, rather than have the adult try to change the students' responses through the teacher's interactions with them.

Again, all of this would appear, at first glance, to be quite well and good. It would seem to be quite obvious that in order to facilitate more effective learning or to better meet young people's needs, either the approach of the teacher or the learning environment itself must change in response to whatever problems are occurring. However, effective as either of these changes might often be in addressing students' learning difficulties or their occasional problematic behavior, merely changing the approach of the teacher or the structure of the environment will often not produce the clarity that will allow more meaningful learning to transpire.

When all is said and done, what serves to truly connect teacher and student, or more closely connect students to both learning environment and subject matter, is a clear understanding of the rights and responsibilities that are possible for both teacher and student in a particular classroom setting.

However, if the educational environment is one in which the adult is the one who usually determines in advance who has what rights and who has what responsibilities in any given situation, then two deleterious dynamics are likely to occur. One is that because the young people themselves are not involved in this determination, they will probably not feel that it is their rights and responsibilities that are being addressed. Rather, they may well come to feel that the rights and responsibilities to which they are expected to acquiesce originate with some vague standards of conduct that have been determined somewhere in the adult world of which they are not a part, rather than from what their own experience tells them is actually transpiring in their classroom setting.

The other dynamic is that it will often be unclear to them what rights and what responsibilities they might potentially have. If appropriate conduct toward both their teacher and their classmates is not a consistently open-ended question that is inherently to be found only in the web of interrelations that transpire in the particular learning environment, then it is not even rights and responsibilities that are being accessed. Instead, it is only external standards of conduct that most often originate with preconceived adult values. The result of this is that because the students in a specific environment are not ferreting rights and responsibilities directly out of their own experience, there is no way that they can possibly know what the potential for each is.

In either of the above cases, young people end up feeling less connected to their learning environment than they otherwise might. If their rights and responsibilities don't actually evolve from their life experiences at school, then they will soon come to experience a genuine disconnect between what they themselves sense is appropriate conduct in relation to their learning and what their teacher has determined in advance this conduct should be. At the same time, they often feel at arm's length from their learning environment simply because it is unclear to them what appropriate conduct might potentially be within that environment.

In other words, if the dividing line between rights and responsibilities is not coming directly from the web of interrelations that adults and young people have established with each other, the young people may very likely come to feel that appropriate conduct is something arbitrary and vague. If this dividing line is instead coming primarily from adult determinations concerning what rights and responsibilities the young people in a particular environment should be accorded, then the issues of fairness and justice—issues that are vitally important to young people—are often experienced by them as being just out of reach.

This is so simply because for young people to feel that they are being treated fairly, they must themselves be involved in determining exactly what is fair and just for all involved. In addition, when young people are denied the opportunity to openly discuss and negotiate what they feel are significant issues, both with their teacher and with their peers, they will very likely come to feel that those issues are being swept under the rug, so to speak. As a result of this, many of the issues that might define appropriate conduct in regard to both learning and behavior will again become vague and uncertain.

Every Thursday morning at 11:30 A.M. at The Children's School, we held a democratic meeting at which everyone in the school, teachers and students alike, sat down together to discuss issues that might affect everyone. During the course of the week, a concern sheet was taped to one of the tables, and anyone could write a concern on it that would be discussed at the meeting. Then, at the beginning of the meeting, the student who was leading the meeting that day read the list of concerns to the entire group, and we all decided, by democratic vote, which issues we wished to discuss first.

These issues involved such things as what consequences should be imposed on students who didn't complete the work on their individual plans by the end of the day, procedures for cleaning the school, the behavior of individual students that was adversely affecting the entire group, what field trips we would be going on, how to better implement the daily schedule, how much time specific teachers or students would be allotted for teaching small group lessons in specific subject matter, and even occasionally discussions of what role the parents should be given in the conduct of certain school affairs.

As one can plainly see, there was very little that was rationalized away. Sometimes, of course, a group of students who were disgruntled with one particular student began to pick on him at a meeting, and so the teachers had to step in. And of course, other issues, such as the amount of recess time students might enjoy, or if specific students or teachers might be dismissed from the school, were not up for a democratic vote, for obvious reasons.

The meetings could sometimes become excruciatingly boring when only superficial issues were being addressed. Other times, they could become quite tense and contentious when concerns grew more personal. However, the ultimate goal was always to try to reach a point of equilibrium in terms of everyone's rights and responsibilities.

Every learning or social situation that might evolve in any classroom possesses certain inherent rights and responsibilities that are necessarily part of the situation itself. There is a certain equilibrium in any situation in which the specific rights and responsibilities of those involved will actually be in balance in relation to each other. So, if a particular individual or group is not acting responsibly, then other peoples' rights are inevitably being violated. Therefore, as much as anything, discussions between teacher and students, or even between students themselves, should involve finding that point of equilibrium where everyone's rights and responsibilities are in balance.

For instance, if a certain teacher is spending her time attempting to teach a student a particular subject matter for which the student has agreed to become responsible and the student is not making a similar effort, then the teacher's rights are being violated. On the other hand, if the teacher is not following through on things like time and materials that he or she has agreed to provide the student for a particular area of learning, then the student's rights are being violated. In addition, of course, there is an equilibrium of rights and responsibilities that exists between a teacher and his or her class of students as a whole, one that often pertains to things like group lessons and social situations.

Trying to reach a point of equilibrium where everyone's rights and responsibilities are balanced does not mean that the students in the environment necessarily have the same capacities, knowledge, and experience that the adults have. Nor does it mean that the adults do not have certain responsibilities owing to the fact that the young people are in their care. What it means is that in any given situation, be it academic or interpersonal, a certain person or group should not have a greater share of the rights and a lesser share of the responsibilities than everyone else.

When this equilibrium of rights and responsibilities is out of balance, then the students in a particular learning environment are inevitably going to feel less connected to it. Young people feel connected to what they are studying and to the environment in which they learn only if they feel they have a certain measure of control over how each is developing. And they feel that they have this measure of control only if their learning, and their relations with the adults in the environment, are evolving out of what is fair and just to all involved. Otherwise, young people feel that they are perpetually at risk of being subjected to the potential capriciousness of adult motives, values, and authority.

Fairness and justice are bottom-line realities with young people when it comes to how willingly they will allow themselves to become involved with other people, or with the particulars of their immediate environment. If they come to feel that others with whom they are involved in certain situations have a greater share of the rights and therefore a lesser share of the responsibilities, they will tend to withdraw from those situations more quickly than most adults will.

Although many adults will remain engaged with a certain situation that they experience as being unfair simply because they have a greater ability to conceptualize exactly what they might attain by staying with the situation, most young people, particularly younger children, have not reached a similar level of inner discipline and maturity. Consequently, they often begin to withdraw from situations and environments that they perceive to be unfair much more quickly, even though they are compelled to physically remain in them.

In fact, more often than educators realize, young people inwardly withdraw from learning situations and environments either because they sense that they have an unequal share of rights relative to the adults who teach them or else the actual rights and responsibilities that they might potentially have are so patently unclear to them. Of course, what often occurs is that this form of withdrawal is confused with a number of other dynamics, such as lack of interest in a particular subject matter or an inability to genuinely connect with one's teachers.

As a result, often the real reason—this unclear dissemination of rights and responsibilities—that an individual student or a group of students does not become more involved with their learning environment is never really addressed. So instead, because it is the more superficial dynamics that are usually being dealt with,

## CHAPTER 7

over time the students in the environment tend to withdraw from it all the more as they come to feel that this genuine need of theirs for clarity is being ignored.

For instance, a student who would like to have greater input into what he is learning but is in a classroom setting where it is never made clear to the students just how much input they might potentially have, will often come to experience the vague sense that there is a better way to connect himself to a certain subject matter. However, he probably won't be able to formulate for himself just what that is because of the complex nature of the relevant dynamics. He will feel that he might be given more latitude concerning how much control over the direction of his learning he might potentially have, but won't be able to fully articulate to himself either why this isn't possible or even what the possibilities for greater involvement are.

As a result, he can't realistically express this concern to his teachers so that this issue can actually be addressed. At the same time, his teachers, who might be stuck in their own preconceptions about adult authority and about the role of the teacher with his or her students, won't be able to begin to address the actual reasons why the student isn't more connected to his learning.

This was something that we were able to do pretty well at The Children's School because of our actual learning environment. Our students were always inquiring of us, in one way or another, how they might approach their learning differently. For instance, if a particular student was becoming frustrated with something on her individual learning plan that she didn't feel was working for her, the matter could be taken up at any time. In other words, she knew that the issue of how much latitude she could be given in meeting certain expectations that she had agreed upon could always be under review.

For example, if students wanted to spread out their learning in a certain subject matter over a longer period of time so that they

## A JUST EQUILIBRIUM

didn't grow tired of the subject, that could be negotiated. If they wanted to learn about something that they had seen on television the night before, it was possible to try to work that into their learning plans. And if they wanted to become part of a group of students that had been learning about something in which they had originally chosen not to become involved but had become interested just by watching the group from across the room, that could also be discussed.

Therefore, because the students felt that they could almost always discuss their academic program, they tended to have a connection to our environment that they almost certainly never would have had if their options in regard to their own learning had been less clear.

The best way for students to clearly recognize what rights and what responsibilities they might have in regard to what they are learning or in regard to their learning environment as a whole is for them to be permitted to discuss all of the manifestations of this issue on an ongoing basis. A balanced equilibrium of rights and responsibilities is something organic that is always changing over time.

As situations change, new factors come into play that change the specific dynamics in a particular situation so that the exact nature of personal rights and responsibilities also changes or else a group of students and teachers becomes aware of the dynamics that are part of the situation that they were not able beforehand to perceive as clearly as they eventually do.

For instance, as students become more engaged by a particular subject matter, new elements can become part of the learning situation, elements that can change the nature of the relationship between teacher and students. These are things like the introduction of more complex materials that require greater direction or more natural authority on the part of the teacher.

On the other hand, the need for more student-directed, hands-on learning activities might be discovered, in which it is important that the adults give the students an adequate amount of room. Or, as much as anything, there are always new students coming into a particular learning environment with different attitudes toward learning and different needs, which will inevitably change the group dynamics concerning rights and responsibilities.

Almost certainly, one of the biggest changes in the equilibrium of rights and responsibilities at The Children's School from year to year was the introduction of new teachers. Some teachers, after arriving, were immediately aware of the sort of horizontal web of equal relations that existed between teacher and students, and so were quickly accepted. Others arrived and either tried to be too controlling with the students, which didn't work at all and led to the students eventually rejecting them, or else they tried to play the role of the movie star teacher who tries to shape student values, which tended to be even worse.

Nevertheless, a new teacher coming into the school always had a dramatic effect on the equilibrium of rights and responsibilities within the general school environment. If the new teacher tended to be stricter with the students than any of the other teachers at the school usually were, then the environment had to move in a certain direction in order to find a new point of equilibrium. What usually occurred, in this case, was that some of the students who had always seen a certain teacher as the disciplinarian in the school tended to relate to that teacher in a more affectionate manner in order to instinctively balance the authority of the new, stricter teacher.

On the other hand, if the new teacher tended to give the students more latitude than the other teachers usually did, then that teacher usually got tested by many of the students in an effort to discover if they could trust him or her to be someone who would really be willing to give them this greater degree of latitude. Then, once that sort of clarity had been achieved, the new social dynamic in the school tended to reach a new point of equilibrium.

## A JUST EQUILIBRIUM

Because the equilibrium of rights and responsibilities in any classroom setting is never fixed but is always evolving, it is essential that teacher and students constantly endeavor, both as a group and on a one-to-one basis, to discuss what is fair and just to all involved in any particular situation. Whether it's a matter of a teacher discussing with his or her class what consequences they think should accrue from unfinished work, or a teacher and student figuring out just what is reasonable for them to expect from each other in exploring a specific subject matter, these kinds of discussions need to become a bottom-line reality if students are to become fully connected to their learning environment.

Otherwise, if the bottom line is the adult authority of the teacher based on adult values and preconceived structures, then the students will not be fully connected to different learning situations. If such is the case, there will always be unanswered questions regarding what the possibilities are for their full and complete participation.

They may feel that they might be given a greater hand in the evolution of a particular situation and also might be given a greater share of the rights and more of the responsibilities. However, if the adult becomes the sole determiner of how that evolution takes place, then those concerns will inevitably be stifled simply because there is no longer a natural equilibrium that everyone is endeavoring to comprehend, respect, and even learn from.

Obviously, as soon as the desire to achieve certain external results, such as good grades or higher test scores, enters a classroom, the basic dynamic between teacher and students tends to move rapidly away from the attempt to achieve that kind of natural equilibrium. If the adult is a figure of authority who gives grades and administers tests as indications of what types of learners individual students are, the adult now holds all the cards.

## CHAPTER 7

In other words, as soon as young people's senses of self-worth in relation to their learning becomes part of an empirical result that is determined by someone else, particularly if it is the sort of vague, amorphous result that grades and test scores tend to be for young people, then their view toward the various rights and responsibilities they might acquire tends to vanish completely.

That is to say, their attention tends to no longer be given to discovering what rights they might be accorded in various learning situations, or clarifying for themselves what they should be responsible for, simply because, in most cases, they now want to do whatever is necessary to achieve the best possible validation of themselves as learners.

Consequently, although they may indeed recognize the basic injustice of certain situations, they now have a more important purpose: to please both adults and themselves with better grades and higher test scores. Therefore, as an outgrowth of this, students will be less connected to their learning environment simply because they are now not as focused on the particular web of interrelations of which they are a part. Achieving certain external results with their learning tends to become more important to them than whether or not certain expectations made of them are fair in relation to those made of other students, or whether all the people in the classroom setting, both teacher and students, are meeting their various responsibilities. And although these latter dynamics will still matter to the students, they will matter increasingly less over time as they become more focused on certain empirical validations of their own learning.

In fact, this is one of the more significant negative effects that giving grades and administering standardized tests has on classroom learning for student in their formative years. It tends to destroy the possibility that there might be a just equilibrium of rights and responsibilities evolving out of the web of interrelations in a particular classroom.

On the other hand, if students are not so concerned with achieving certain grades and test scores, and personal accountability for one's learning becomes the bottom-line reality, then the issue of rights and responsibilities tends to return to center stage. Now the standards and expectations for learning that individual students have developed with their teacher are soon fully perceived by the other students in relation to their own standards and expectations.

Consequently, the issues of fairness and justice now come to be significantly more important simply because the students' focus has now moved away from attaining the empirical validations and external rewards for their learning that grades and test scores are. Instead, it has now moved toward a desire to know that one's rights and responsibilities in relation to one's own learning are being established fairly in relation to other students' rights and responsibilities. As an outgrowth of this, then, the students will tend to instinctively seek out what they consider to be a just equilibrium in any particular learning-related situation.

Educational environments that give young people the opportunity to have a significant voice in determining what rights and what responsibilities accrue from different situations are healthy environments primarily because they are based on guidance, not unnatural adult authority. That is, because the students are themselves involved in the determination of where the dividing line is in any situation between rights and responsibilities, they will inherently be given more personal space in making their own decisions concerning how they might best utilize instruction from adults. As a result, their learning remains more firmly in their own hands.

When students are given the latitude to determine how classroom situations in which they find themselves will actually evolve because they have themselves negotiated the bottom-line issues of fairness and justice, young people will then be able to employ

CHAPTER 7

these issues as guideposts in making effective use of their learning environment. In addition, because they are no longer so dependent upon unnatural adult authority, bolstered by certain empirical validations of learning, to direct them, they will tend to be much more connected to their learning and to their learning environment as a whole.

All learning has an interpersonal, social aspect to it. Whether it's a single teacher teaching a class of thirty students or a student and teacher working together on a one-to-one basis, the issues of fairness and justice are inevitably going to be a part of the situation, whether those involved want to realistically address them or not.

To ensure that different learning situations are clear to the students involved, so that they can best connect themselves to the learning situations, it is important that teachers and students bring the issue of rights and responsibilities fully out into the open and negotiate it on a consistent basis. Otherwise, unclear apprehensions and vague ideas concerning the equilibrium of rights and responsibilities inherent in any learning situation inevitably cause students to feel less connected to it.

There are always times when the adults have to make decisions concerning what transpires in the learning environment for which they are ultimately responsible. After all, the young people are in their care. However, what is of equal importance is that those students are given the opportunity to consistently clarify for themselves the learning situations in which they are involved by working with their teachers to ascertain just where the point of equilibrium between rights and responsibilities lies; that is really the best way for them to be fully connected to the environment in which they learn.

So far, the debate over the long-term effects that the current testing culture in our schools is having upon young people has been centered largely on whether or not it is facilitating more effective learning; this is certainly a debate worth having. However, what is almost never addressed when the effects that high-stakes, standardized tests and the seemingly increasing obsession with attaining good grades are discussed is how these things tend to rule out from their inception the possibility that interactions between teachers and students might become more democratic.

When young people are not only so easily influenced but actually shaped by the messages that adults send them about themselves, and when a young person's sense of himself or herself as a learner is largely determined by external results that are entirely in the hands of adults, then young people are very much at the mercy of these empirical validations. Their basic relationship with their teachers now becomes one of genuine subservience rather than of equal partnership. As a result of this, students tend to become less connected to the object of their learning and to the learning environment as a whole.

Learning in order to achieve certain external results that are not only determined by somebody else but are also not part of standards that the student has had a hand in creating is probably the best way there is to create learning environments that young people feel are inherently unfair and unjust, whether they openly express this concern or not. In our present results-driven culture, this is indeed the bottom-line, unaddressed question lurking in the shadows; it is ultimately going to have long-term consequences for students' learning and also for contemporary learning environments.

# 8

# THE STUDENT'S OWN EXPERIENCE

The best environment for students in their formative years is one in which their learning evolves directly from their personal experience. That is to say, their learning does not originate with rigidly preconceived philosophies or methodologies; with predetermined, adult-generated curriculums; or with approaches born of adult values, which are all unnecessarily imposed on young people by the adults who are their teachers.

Rather, the best environment proceeds from young people having a significant hand in creating their own learning progressions, from genuine needs that are not falsely created in them, and from the strength of their own impressions. In addition, it is significantly based upon important developmental concerns and on students being directly involved in ascertaining the rights and responsibilities that are inherent to specific learning situations. In addition, students' learning that stems from their own experience is not judged primarily by adults according to external standards that would cause young people to steer their learning in pursuit of those extrinsic rewards.

# CHAPTER 8

If learning and personal experience are to be bound together in the student as a singular process, then this path must be open ended. The day-to-day experience of the young person as he or she learns, in all of its various manifestations, must be what essentially determines the direction of such learning—and not the preconceived, externally imposed structures and approaches aimed at achieving particular empirical results.

Otherwise, such structures and approaches will eventually cause students' learning to move in one direction while their personal experience of learning situations proceeds in another direction. Eventually, as this process becomes more and more of an entrenched reality, learning will come to be experienced by young people as something that necessarily exists outside the bounds of their own curiosities, interests, needs, and impulses.

The preceding, as much as anything, has been an exposition of the ways in which our contemporary, results-driven culture not only prevents young people from becoming firmly grounded in the dynamics of their own experiences as they learn but also dangerously separates learning and personal experience in them as two separate processes.

Furthermore, these damaging things happen not because anyone wishes for them to occur; they happen simply because we have created learning environments that guarantee, regardless of what educators might do, that these adverse effects will take place. In other words, the manner in which the dynamics of young people's experiences evolve is utterly dependent upon the educational milieu in which those experiences take place.

Competent, caring teachers can certainly foster, within the parameters of the particular learning environment, curiosity, learning, and a certain amount of healthy personal development in the students they teach. Yet what teachers cannot do is to assist those students in becoming more grounded in their own experience as they learn if the environment in which they teach is not geared to allow them to do that. For instance, teachers may be able to genuinely interest their students in the details of specific subject matter. However, if they are also required to give the students grades, the teachers will be powerless to prevent how those grades take the students outside their own experience in a disembodied manner as they learn the particular subject.

Teachers might encourage their students to always ask questions about what they are learning. However, if they are teaching according to adult-generated, predetermined learning progressions that the students in their classes have had no real hand in creating, their learning and personal experience will begin to dangerously separate from each other when the students are unable to develop any significant point of view toward the knowledge they are assimilating.

Or teachers might present their students with well-organized, attractive information and interesting lessons by which they can assimilate that information. However, if the curricula that their school employs are developed primarily to achieve certain test scores and are also, in conjunction with this, based on rigid timetables for learning, then it is inevitable that the inner lives of those students will be significantly dulled when they aren't able to spend enough time with any strong impressions that they may be experiencing.

Or teachers might be interesting, caring, and thoughtful. However, if any of their students have developmental issues that they haven't been able to resolve because of their rigid daily schedules, those students won't be able to become fully grounded in their academic learning.

How young people's education is going to affect them has much more to do with the learning environment in which they find themselves than with anything else. Teachers who are not able—largely, these days, due to the need by their school to achieve certain results on high-stakes, standardized tests—to set

CHAPTER 8

up their environments in a way that allows their students to fully connect to them are inevitably going to reap exactly what they sow: students who become increasingly mistrustful of, and alienated from, their own experience and learning because they are not able to consistently complete them.

However, in order to provide learning environments that do indeed facilitate this healthy completion of experience, a number of probing questions concerning the function of education in our society have to be addressed. Foremost among them is the question of what is real learning. Is it simply the accumulation of facts, knowledge, and skills, or is it something much more than just that? If, ultimately, genuine learning and personal experience are both part of the very same experiential flow, then this question and its possible answers become considerably more complex. In that case, one must think in terms of how to facilitate the assimilation of knowledge and skills while allowing learners to remain fully grounded in their own experiences as they do so.

Yet, to properly understand this issue, one must in fact look squarely at the damaging effects that the conditioning of young people's experiences in their formative years, as they learn, has on their future development. In fact, in conjunction with our current obsession over standardized test scores, this may well be the reason we have evolved the sort of rigid, superficial, unfocused approaches to education that are employed in so many of our schools. We're just not aware of the extent of the dangers inherent in setting up learning environments that do not actually facilitate healthy experiential dynamics.

Young people who are learning in a manner that causes them to become mistrustful of what their experience tells them can often be at the beginning of a lifelong, irreversible process that leads toward their becoming a more superficial person than what they might have otherwise eventually become. We tend not to think much about how, once children's impressions become

THE STUDENT'S OWN EXPERIENCE

dulled during their formative years, they are in danger of living the rest of their lives with a dulled awareness. Nor are we as aware as we should be about how the creation of false needs in young people, due to adult preconceptions about them, can often set them on a singular, wrong course toward becoming someone whom they are not actually meant to become.

These are just some of the dangers inherent in employing predetermined structures to set up educational environments to which young people have to adapt themselves by learning to impede, mistrust, or narrow their experience. If one is looking squarely at these dangers, not just with one's mind but also with one's heart, one must ask: Is what is gained in the bargain really worth it?

Learning plans and curricula that are carefully conceived by educators to ensure that certain information, facts, and skills are acquired by students at a certain point in time may indeed serve to focus the attention of those students on the relevant knowledge that it is important for them to acquire. However, if young people's learning and personal experience begin to dangerously separate from each other when the young people are given no significant say in determining how they approach such knowledge, is it worth it?

Good grades and high test scores may indeed give young people feelings of self-confidence and serve to motivate them. However, if those grades and test scores set up a pattern within the students of being motivated to learn for some reason that is external to the learning itself so that genuine learning seldom continues to reside completely in the students' minds and curiosities, are they worth it?

Academic standards of accountability that are in place in order to ensure that students in a certain age group are not lagging behind the other students in that age grouping might indeed give young people a somewhat better opportunity to compete with

CHAPTER 8

their chronological peers. However, if those standards cause teachers to focus so exclusively on achieving certain empirical results that they do not have the time or inclination to assist students with developmental concerns that need to be addressed before their learning can become truly meaningful to them, are they worth it?

Thoughtful, consistent, well-structured approaches that focus on empirical results and external accountability may indeed make it more certain that students will acquire certain information, knowledge, and skills by a particular point in time. However, if those same approaches also stem from adult preconception about young people's needs that don't allow teachers to perceive and then meet the actual needs of young people in a particular school, then are they worth it?

With the present trend in education being one of looking at higher scores on standardized tests as some sort of holy grail, particularly when school funding and teacher accountability have become so inextricably linked to those scores, we are presently moving ever further away from looking seriously at the sorts of issues concerning young people's experience that have been posed here.

If we continue to focus so exclusively on empirical results of academic learning, then it seems almost certain that we will concern ourselves less and less with the dynamics of healthy experience in students as they learn. There really doesn't seem to be any way to resolve this contradiction, in large measure because we have yet to develop a coherent approach to the education of students in their formative years that unites significant attention to healthy experiential dynamics with meaningful learning.

However, in order to develop such an approach in our schools, it would seem that the first thing that we must do is to eliminate any unnecessary ingredients from learning situations that prevent young people from being firmly grounded in their own experience as they learn. Anything that is not part of a student's attempt to make genuine contact with a subject area or learning situation will tend to stand in the way of the student having the opportunity to complete his or her experience in relation to it.

Ulterior motives for learning adopted by adults and that lie outside the learning situation itself will stand in the way. False or incomplete images of students formed by their teachers will stand in the way. Learning that is pushed too rapidly along a particular continuum so that young people cannot impressionistically absorb what is in front of them will stand in the way. Unresolved developmental issues that find their way into the learning situation will stand in the way. And, of course, overly rigid scheduling of time-based learning will always stand in the way between students and what they are attempting to assimilate.

The best kind of learning always takes place when there are no extraneous dynamics present in the learning situation, lurking in the background to unduly influence it. Then there is only a fully involved teacher, a fully involved student, and the subject area itself. However, if the types of results-driven approaches and structures alluded to in previous chapters continue to exist in our schools, this sort of optimal learning situation has very little, if any, chance of coming into existence with any degree of regularity.

Unfortunately, young people's learning has become inextricably linked with these approaches and structures simply because of our present confusion of results that are derived empirically with what it genuinely means to be a successful learner. One hears constantly these days about schools that have "turned themselves around" or are now "quality schools" simply because their students score higher on certain high-stakes, standardized tests. Indeed, more and more, successful learning is entirely equated with scoring at a certain level on these tests.

## CHAPTER 8

Consequently, the need by many classroom teachers and other educators to produce certain results on these tests has led them to structure learning environments increasingly in advance of young people even arriving in them, something that is nothing short of a compulsion that seems to get ever stronger over time. However, what seems to have been lost in all the fear and confusion over trying to be certain that students and teachers are successful with these external validations of learning is one simple fact: Teachers can actually engender solid, meaningful learning by simply beginning with the concerns, needs, and interests of their individual students, and then just move from there.

Of course, teachers have to be aware of the specific subject areas and skills they need to introduce to their students. They also have to be aware of just how they can assess whether or not those students are learning and making progress. However, if they are careful, they can keep anything out of the learning situation that stands between students and teacher, or between students and subject matter.

This we tried to do at The Children's School by not bringing any hidden agendas to the learning situation, whether they involved a single student or a group of students. And in order to do this, more than anything, we tried to maintain a genuine reality of encounter between teachers and students. Just the fact that teachers and students were on a first-name basis with each other, and actually related to each other in these terms, meant that when adults and young people sat down to work together, the focus was nearly always on the subject matter in front of them and not on hidden motives, agendas, and misleading images.

Yes, this led at times to students feeling free to become upset in a manner that led to the interruption of certain lessons, mainly because relations between teachers and students tended to be much more informal and personal than they might have been in many other schools. However, the realization by students that teachers were coming to lessons with them as the human beings they really were, warts and all, meant that the students could feel more comfortable in focusing on a particular subject matter as the sole object of their concerns, rather than focusing on adult motives and agendas.

More than anything, our most important concern in educating students in their formative years should be keeping any unnecessary elements out of optimal, pristine learning situations whose primary characteristic is that they contain nothing except for teacher, learner, and subject area. Even if one teacher is simultaneously teaching a number of students a single subject, it is still possible to keep the learning situation healthy, pure, and free from the damaging effects that have been previously discussed in this work.

The first thing that can be done in regard to this is for teachers and other educators to change their mind-set from one of being primarily implementers and representatives of methods of instruction aimed primarily at achieving certain external results, and instead become, to a much greater degree, students of human experience. And yes, of course, there are many teachers in our schools who are acutely aware of the anxieties, needs, and motivations of their students. However, what is being alluded to here is a much broader, more far-reaching attention to the dynamics of their individual students' experience so that teachers can actually begin to build their approaches and learning environments upon exactly these.

In order to accomplish this, however, teachers of students in their formative years would need to be willing to take the seemingly radical step of beginning each school year with no approach or curriculum aimed at achieving certain external results rigidly in place, and then carefully construct approaches to learning, bit by bit, out of what the actual experiential dynamics of their individual students have to offer them—that is, out of the truths that

## CHAPTER 8

their perceptions of, and interactions with, their students on a daily basis yields to them.

Curricula for both individual students and for groups of students can be developed by simply negotiating learning plans with students that evolve from their needs and interests—and not from the need to achieve a certain predetermined, empirical result—and then holding both students and teachers accountable for what they said they were going to do. This is exactly what we did at The Children's School. One doesn't need either predetermined curricula or grades and tests scores in order to do this. A teacher can simply begin by assessing what the academic needs of his or her students are, negotiate learning plans with them for meeting those needs, and then develop and implement teaching strategies in accordance with those learning plans.

Of course, teachers should always be responsible for bringing, and having the right to bring, to the learning environment any lessons or subject areas that they think their students might either have an interest in or else need to acquire for the development of their general knowledge or academic skills. However, the exact manner in which that information or development of skills finds its way into the learning environment can evolve out of the needs and interests of their individual students.

Again, as we tried to do at The Children's School, the nature and structure of the school day itself can evolve organically from the different learning styles, developmental needs, and academic interests of the students by developing schedules and structures that allow them, whenever possible, to be fully present in any learning situation in which they are engaged. That is, structuring of lessons that allow students to develop their own learning progressions; factoring time into the day for them to deal with interpersonal, developmental concerns; or permitting them to remain with any aspects of their learning that are engendering strong impressions within them are just some of the ways to accomplish this.

## THE STUDENT'S OWN EXPERIENCE

One doesn't need either preconceived approaches and curricula aimed at producing certain empirical results or rigidly scheduled school days in order to do this. In fact, these things will often end up getting in the way because of all the reasons mentioned earlier in this work.

What one does need is consistent, honest, insightful observations of students as one is teaching them and not the sorts of observations in which those students are viewed through the particular prism of whatever preconceived approach a certain school is employing. Instead, what is needed is for the teacher to carefully observe each student's needs and tendencies out of the relationship with him or her that is a true reality of encounter.

What this means is that, within the context of any particular learning situation, both student and teacher are experiencing each other purely and directly as the individual people that they are. The teacher is not bringing the agenda of some administrator, school board, or some predetermined methodology to the learning situation, nor is the teacher bringing any sort of false persona or unnecessary position of authority that he or she needs to employ to present those agendas. The teacher is not even bringing a preconceived idea or image of what a teacher is supposed to be, but simply bringing himself or herself as the person he or she actually is, and from that reality of encounter the teacher engages the students in a particular subject matter.

That is the only way to be certain that teachers are accurately observing their students. As soon as something that is extraneous to the learning situation becomes part of it—whether it be predetermined approaches, mandated curricula, exterior agendas, or external evaluations—then it is almost inevitable that teachers will begin to form images of their students that emanate from those external realities.

Teachers who are teaching solely according to a specific preconceived philosophy or methodology that embodies what are

# CHAPTER 8

believed to be certain truths concerning how students best learn or about what their healthy development entails will almost certainly begin to form images of their students that have to do with how well the students do or do not embody those supposed truths. In the process, teachers will often not comprehend something about a particular student that does not stem from the preconceived approach.

Therefore, if teachers in our schools are going to develop approaches, curricula, or daily schedules out of their unclouded observations of the needs of their students, rather than be forced to develop these prior to their experience with them, it is extremely important that anything that might cause teachers to develop preconceived images of their students be kept out of the learning situation.

This truly experiential approach to educating students in their formative years, in which a teacher simply begins with the observations of, and experience with, the students, and moves increasingly outward from there toward intelligent approaches, methods, and curricula rather than vice versa, is something that can be implemented in any classroom, either public or private, as long as one is willing to carefully construct it, piece by piece, from the actual experience of the students in that classroom and not beforehand from adult preconceptions aimed primarily at achieving predetermined results.

One of the major problems that we face in our schools and classrooms today is simply that the basic learning situation that includes teacher, student, and subject matter has become so absurdly complex. One can almost be certain now that whenever a teacher sits down to teach a single student, or else appears in front of either a full class or small group of students, there are so many layers of test-oriented hidden agendas, preconceived structural details, or unnecessary time constraints that the possibility of teacher and student actually approaching the essential purity of connecting with each other and with a specific subject matter, with nothing getting in the way, is almost nonexistent.

Nowhere more than when applied to the education of students in their formative years is the old adage "less is more" more relevant. Consequently, what needs to be a major challenge of an education of the future is to simply regain the essential purity of the basic learning situation involving student, teacher, and subject matter. However, this cannot happen if contemporary elementary and middle schools, and even in some cases high schools, continue to employ a mind-set in which the personal experience of the learner is both shaped and defined by educational structures in which a student's experience and learning are increasingly predetermined and controlled in order to achieve certain empirical results.

It is certainly not being said here that significant learning by students, for which both they and their teachers are accountable, should not take place. Instead, what is being said is that there are many unnecessary entities in our schools that can be dispensed with in order that student and teacher become more fully connected and so that students become more connected to specific areas of learning.

Many of these have already been discussed in previous chapters; the great majority of them have to do with our current obsession with grades and with the results of high-stakes, standardized tests.

They include, among other things, predetermined, mandated curricula developed by organizations and people other than the actual teacher who has to implement them; inflexibly quantified determinations of student progress, rather than more genuine anecdotal or narrative assessments; overly structured school days that make so few allowances for young people either pursuing unique interests or for resolving authentic developmental needs; and rigid timetables for learning that are becoming ever more tied to national standards of evaluation, which ultimately affect school funding.

Certainly, all of these things have been criticized before, yet they are nearly always criticized primarily because their critics believe that they stand in the way of students becoming more effective learners, which is often true. However, what seldom seems to be mentioned is the danger that these sorts of approaches and structures are to the healthy evolution of young people's personal experience itself, and the actual damage that they tend to do to such evolution. Primary among this damage is the manner in which young people are so seldom allowed to complete their own experience.

The evils that so many schools perpetrate on the development in students of healthy experiential dynamics all have to do, in one form or another, with fostering incomplete experiences. These experiences range from students not being given the time or assistance needed to develop a genuine point of view toward what they are learning; to not being given the personal space that is often necessary to either experience their germinating impressions to their fullest possible extent or else to fully resolve interpersonal, developmental issues; to not being organically connected to their learning environments, or to most subject matter, because they have had so little hand in the construction of either one. All of these things cause the sort of damage they do simply because they stand in the way of young people fully completing their experience.

Furthermore, when completion of experience does not take place in young people, either cognitively or developmentally, this not only stifles both their mental and personal development in a neurotic fashion, but it also sets up a pattern in their lives in which they habitually begin to shortchange themselves in terms of how far and how fully they might pursue what is transpiring inside themselves.

## THE STUDENT'S OWN EXPERIENCE

There is a way to address this potential danger and to try to keep it from occurring, and this is to simply begin to pare away in our schools anything that stands in the way of students and teachers fully connecting with subject matter and with each other. Only then, out of this sort of full partnership, can approaches to learning and learning environments themselves be organically created by young people and adults working together—approaches that are open ended enough to allow for the full evolution of student experience.

However, it is hard to see how this can possibly occur if we continue to necessarily equate empirical results with successful learning. In our present climate, we are in danger of not only doing that but of also beginning to completely dissolve any distinction whatsoever between what educators and students might see as successful learning and adult-conceived empirical evaluations of that learning.

Successful learning is nearly always a process that originates and proceeds from the natural curiosity and impressions of the learner. If young people become conditioned to learn in order to achieve certain grades or test scores early in their lives, the type of learning that proceeds directly from the natural interests of the learner is not only being impeded, but it is often being negated altogether.

In the final analysis, creating better schools has as much to do with eliminating what isn't necessary and what is in fact damaging to the evolution of healthy experiential dynamics in young people as it does with anything else. Yes, certainly one of the difficulties to be overcome is the number of students that one teacher has to teach at a particular time. Obviously, high student-to-teacher ratios add many layers of structure, control, and depersonalization to the learning situation, measures that might not be necessary with fewer students in a classroom.

## CHAPTER 8

However, that is still not the real problem. The real problem is that in the creation of our schools we have failed to ask the most fundamental of questions regarding human development and learning: How does the experience of young people (i.e., the manner in which they make increasing contact with their world) evolve in a healthy manner as they learn? What sort of learning milieu will facilitate this healthy evolution, and what sort of milieu and structure will suppress it?w

How might the dynamics of healthy personal experience and academic learning be conjoined as a single process? And how can adult knowledge, expertise, and life experience be brought to the learning situation so that these things facilitate, guide, and direct young people with their learning in a way that does not also suppress, shape, or condition their personal development in an unhealthy manner?

If we're really going to improve how young people are educated in our society, we have to begin by becoming better students of their experiential dynamics. We have to make this the primary ingredient in establishing proper learning environments. Otherwise, the personal experience of many students will continue to evolve in an increasingly neurotic fashion as they learn. Students in their formative years can learn effectively and meaningfully while also growing in a developmentally healthy manner only if those two things come to be seen by us, their parents and teachers, as one and the same process.

# DIAGNOSIS AND EVALUATION

Certainly, it is important that classroom teachers have a clear idea of the progress that their students are making in acquiring various knowledge and skills. In conjunction with this, it is also important that they have reliable diagnostic procedures at their disposal that give them as clear a picture as possible of this progress.

There is certainly nothing wrong with using specific evaluations that employ certain empirical standards in order to determine both student strengths and weaknesses in different subject areas. In such cases, teachers, because they have become more aware through these procedures of exactly which skills and knowledge their students may be lacking, can more effectively give those students both the specific type and also the proper amount of direction that they require.

Unfortunately, the difficulty that tends to come into play with these evaluations and standards is when they are used in some sort of judgmental fashion, as they increasingly are in our current results-driven culture. Procedures that were originally designed

## CHAPTER 9

so that teachers might effectively diagnose certain areas of difficulty that students were having with their learning are now being increasingly used to simply label teachers, students, and schools as being successes or failures. As was mentioned in an earlier chapter, empirical test scores are rapidly becoming entirely the standard by which everyone is judged.

Therefore, what is now occurring as teachers and schools not only continue to teach to the test but in fact create whole curriculums in an effort to achieve certain test scores, is that the learning process itself is being increasingly removed from the hands of both students and teachers. That is exactly what confusing diagnosis of learning with judgment of learning does. First, this confusion sends a powerful message to young people that because they are being judged by adults according to their strengths and weaknesses as learners rather than having these strengths and weaknesses discovered by adults primarily as a means to assist the students in becoming more effective learners, the real point of their learning is mainly that of pleasing those adults who evaluate them.

Second, it puts teachers who might use evaluative procedures, such as certain standardized tests, primarily as a means of discovering specifically with what areas their students might need more assistance in the position of instead using these procedures mainly to produce the best results, rather than simply using them to ascertain how they might give their students the direction that they might require.

As a consequence of this, it is inevitable that many teachers will end up designing their curriculums to produce higher test scores in certain areas, instead of using the procedures diagnostically to meet the needs of individual students. Then, as the diagnostic aspects of these evaluative procedures become increasingly less important, classroom teachers won't be able to use them as effectively to discover those areas with which their students need greater direction.

## DIAGNOSIS AND EVALUATION

Teaching to the test is not really teaching at all. It is merely training young people to reproduce certain information and knowledge on which they will be evaluated without genuinely considering their unique individual needs as learners. Yes, of course, they may indeed be taught certain information, knowledge, and skills—but it will be the sort of teaching in which, because teachers are so focused on their students achieving certain empirical results, they focus less and less on diagnosing their individual needs.

It is indeed possible to use a certain standardized test to ascertain specifically what skills and knowledge a student may be lacking. In fact, the Iowa Test of Basic Skills, for example, can be effectively used to discover skill levels of students in specific areas in both mathematics and language arts. Furthermore, if teachers employ it in that context, to look at results in order to see what specific skills an individual student may need assistance with, the test itself can actually serve a valuable purpose.

However, as soon as the judgmental aspects of these types of empirical assessments enter the picture, then the results of these evaluations tend to have the deleterious effects on young people alluded to earlier in this work. That is, educators today often tend to take those results and either develop entire curriculums around them or else limit the type of direction that they give their students to what they believe in the future will allow those students to produce the best test scores.

As a consequence of this, teachers are now directing young people's learning in order that they might produce better results with the specific evaluative procedures that were originally designed to diagnose student strengths and weaknesses so that the teacher could be more effective at helping them become better learners.

So now the original purpose of these evaluative procedures—to determine how classroom teachers can better assist their students

## CHAPTER 9

with specific subject areas—has been subverted in favor of a judgmental approach in which students actually learn in order to produce better empirical results. And the reason that this false approach that produces increasingly less meaningful learning in students, and less efficient direction by their teachers, exists is not so very hard to determine. It is simply that diagnosis has now been replaced by judgment.

Again, there is certainly nothing wrong with diagnosing students' learning in order to ascertain how their teachers might more effectively direct them. Teachers look at the specific areas in which young people have been evaluated and then use what they find to design learning plans, in which the students are involved, that will assist the students in acquiring certain knowledge and skills they may be lacking. When that is what is being done, there is a natural, meaningful progression from diagnosis to adult assistance to more efficient learning.

However, once teachers begin to use the results of certain evaluations to skew the students' curricula so that teachers can produce better scores the next time the students are tested, this natural progression from diagnosis to direction becomes completely turned on its head. Now the teachers are designing curricula for their students that will direct their attention and learning toward certain predetermined results. As a consequence of this, teachers will often not be able to diagnose certain strengths and weaknesses that might have been discovered if the students had been evaluated in a more open-ended manner.

If teachers are attempting to honestly evaluate what the specific strengths and weaknesses are for various students, this will be much harder to do if a particular subject matter is reduced to those aspects of it that will most likely produce the most favorable test results. In that case, if certain strengths or weaknesses of specific students exist outside this particular field of information, they are likely to be overlooked.

## DIAGNOSIS AND EVALUATION

At The Children's School, because we didn't employ standardized testing to evaluate students, only two things ever really determined where the direction of students' learning would gravitate: the natural sequence of a particular learning progression and a student's own interests and curiosities. Consequently, there was never any sort of external consideration that forced the flow of such leaning in an unnatural direction, such as the desire for higher test scores by the student and teacher.

What this often did for both students and teachers was to keep a certain, often unspoken, pressure that exists in many other schools, and that relates to the need to attain better test scores, out of both individual and group lessons and out of the learning environment altogether. Consequently, two positive things resulted from this. One was that the relations between teachers and students could be more genuine simply because there wasn't the ever-present agenda of attaining higher test scores lurking in the background to poison such relations.

The other consequence, which was probably even more significant, was that because students and teachers at our school didn't feel a need to skew learning and lessons in a particular direction for the purpose of attaining certain predetermined, empirical test results, there could be an actual continuity present in both lessons and in the overall school environment. Students could pursue interests and curiosities with a significantly lessened fear of interruption. Teachers could take the time to pursue occasional learning that resulted when certain students wished to temporarily address interests and curiosities that were incidental to the prescribed lesson.

In addition, because there was not the constant pressure to stay on whatever track led to greater preparation for high-stakes, standardized testing, teachers and students could often take the time to negotiate the issue of rights and responsibilities and of how to generate a more just learning environment. As a result,

CHAPTER 9

students were often able to remain more connected to their learning, and to the overall learning environment, than they would have been able to be if the need to stay focused on the exclusive academic learning that leads toward higher test scores had caused us to continually sweep the issues of fairness and justice under the rug.

When tools that should be employed to assist teachers in becoming more effective in giving their students the type of direction they require are used primarily to judge both teacher and student, then disembodied, disinterested learning is sure to follow. In that event, students and teachers are less concerned with the natural flow of learning that should be based largely on the learner's curiosities, impressions, natural interests, and needs. Instead, both young people and adults become increasingly focused on how to point that learning in a direction that will yield certain empirical results of evaluations that were originally designed to be used diagnostically.

This confusion of diagnosis with judgment is very much at the heart of why our present results-driven culture often does so much damage to the inner lives of young people. When evaluative procedures that should be used primarily to diagnose difficulties, and in so doing assist students in becoming better learners, are used judgmentally, then the facilitation of healthy experiential dynamics in the learner is an issue that is often ignored.

Once teachers begin to make judgments about students' capacities as learners based on empirical results of certain evaluations, and about their own abilities as a teacher that are also judged according to them, then the students' learning is going to be inevitably skewed away from assisting them with what is transpiring inside them as they learn. Instead, teachers and students will tend to focus exclusively on simply achieving the best possible external results. As a consequence of this, the paths of the students' learning and their viewpoints on what learning actually entails are now being shaped in a manner that encourages young people to learn in the increasingly disembodied manner alluded to in earlier chapters.

One can understand why, as students apply to colleges and professional schools, it becomes necessary to evaluate their learning in a certain judgmental fashion. However, to replace diagnosis with evaluation so thoroughly in the lives of young people in their formative years, as we are increasingly doing, is something that has to be questioned. Even the argument that empirical test results can be used to determine whether teachers and schools are providing their students with the skills and knowledge they need to acquire has its inherent flaws.

As anyone who has spent time as a classroom teacher administering standardized tests to students in their formative years knows, the results of those tests are often significantly at variance with students' actual abilities in certain areas. Often this has to do with certain students' inability to focus for long periods of time in testing situations, or with their genuine lack of interest in achieving certain scores. In particular, these things obviously tend to be true of younger children.

Of course, a much better indication of how well students are learning is the classroom teacher's day-to-day experience in teaching them specific subject matter, and the teacher can certainly keep highly specific records having to do with learning specific skills or acquiring certain knowledge. For example, if at the end of the school year, a younger student is having difficulty decoding certain phonemes in learning to read, or borrowing and carrying numbers between numerical hierarchies, this can certainly be noted in a way in which his or her teacher the following year will know exactly where to start in teaching the young student to read or work with numbers.

Quite simply, replacing what should be basic diagnostic procedures with empirical, judgmental evaluations of student progress

CHAPTER 9

over time tends to be a tried-and-true way to create problems with the experiential dynamics of young people in their formative years that are related to their learning. However, if this issue is going to be realistically addressed, then the entire educational establishment must begin by disentangling monies for school funding from empirical test scores to which they are often so rigidly tied.

There is a certain false premise inherent in allocating so much money in terms of external evaluations that often give one only a limited idea of what is occurring in the life and learning of a student. Much more significantly, once the very existence of schools becomes dependent upon funds that are allocated in this manner, then the results of empirical evaluations inevitably shape and control the paths that young people take with their learning in a manner that ignores many of their important experiential dynamics.

However, because money tends to so quickly become a bottom-line reality in the existence of contemporary schools, it needs to be tied instead to alternative standards that will not result in the damage to the inner lives of young people that is the subject of this work. And yet, if those standards are to be more anecdotal and personal in nature, and to remain essentially in the hands of classroom teachers, then something else must change. Monies that are distributed to schools should be distributed by those who make more of an effort to determine what is actually occurring within the classrooms of a particular school, instead of being allocated by those in state and local government who rely so thoroughly, and often so blindly, on the results of high-stakes, standardized tests.

In a private school, if parents no longer trust that the teachers are doing an adequate job of educating their children, they can simply remove them from the school. There is often a direct connection between monies that a school accrues by tuition and the quality of education that the students in the school are receiving.

## DIAGNOSIS AND EVALUATION

However, in a public school, the state, which provides a school with its funding, acts as a middleman of sorts between parents and educators, attempting to be certain that the children of those parents are learning as well as they might. So, of course, because those who represent the state are not present in a particular school on any sort of daily basis, they end up relying almost exclusively on test scores to make such an evaluation.

This might indeed be a reliable method if it were not for three significant factors. One is that there are simply any number of students in any school who simply don't test well. For whatever reason—nerves, lack of interest in the testing situation or in how well they perform, or the need to think outside the box—their test scores are not an accurate reflection of their actual competencies in a particular subject area.

The second factor is that there are any number of students being tested in a particular school who may not have acquired all the information or knowledge on which they are being tested by committing it to memory—yet they are still able to not only retrieve such information or knowledge when they need it, using the Internet or other means, but also have a good idea of how to apply it to relevant areas of the particular subject matter, to other subject matters, or to the world outside the schoolhouse door.

In this regard, one thinks immediately of students who might not have committed to memory the different parts of speech or are still unsure of such things as how to properly use a semicolon, but are still fluent writers whose ability to write is tied holistically to high-level verbal or reading skills. And as far as learning to punctuate sentences effectively, there is of course always the processor inside one's computer that can come to one's assistance whenever needed.

The third factor that makes it often difficult to equate certain standardized test scores with adequate learning is that occasionally there are certain highly intelligent students who have a much broader view of a particular subject area than the specific material on which they are tested.

At The Children's School, we periodically administered the Iowa Test of Basic Skills to students who were leaving us for high school. Several different times, we were able to observe students who already had a genuine acquaintance with different aspects of theoretical physics—the basic nature of both quantum mechanics and relativity theory—not score particularly well on the science part of the test that essentially tested the basic scientific knowledge that they had already moved past, and so no longer had much relevance for them.

We also saw students who were already familiar with algebra, or even in a couple of cases basic calculus, not score well on the mathematics section of the test that was time based. And because the students at our school were not familiar with the time-based learning put in place in many schools to ensure that students will acquire all the knowledge and competencies they need in order to test well, this part of the test was often not reflective of the actual level of their ability in mathematics.

Any number of big-city school systems are now run by businessmen and -women, functioning primarily as CEOs, rather than by professionally trained educators. This trend, unfortunately, means that many of those school systems have now replaced the idea of the individual student being educated according to the student's unique needs with what amounts to an employer/worker model of education. It also means that we are moving perilously closer to a mind-set in which evaluation and judgment are now thoroughly replacing diagnosis and individual assistance.

In fact, if one looks more closely at this trend, this is really an alarming indication that schools increasingly exist primarily not to educate the individual student as a whole person, but rather that the student essentially exists in the school atmosphere so that he or she can have his or her competencies judged by society as a whole. Although some may believe that this is a rather specious definition that splits hairs, as far as the basic message imparted to many students regarding the essential nature of their education, it is anything but that.

Even though most students in their formative years aren't able to actually formulate in words to themselves that their school environment feels more impersonal to them than it otherwise might, much less comprehend the reasons why this is so, there is a definite message being sent to them, a message that steadily flows into the classroom setting when schools begin running more like businesses than as schools: The student is primarily there to please the adults, rather than vice versa. As a consequence, young people feel increasingly less ownership over their learning.

In the final analysis, we as educators have to realize that we simply cannot have it both ways. Either we are primarily concerned with using diagnostic procedures in a nonjudgmental manner in order to facilitate a healthy, efficient approach to learning that is essentially concerned with what transpires within a student as he or she learns, or we are concerned with conditioning young people's learning and personal experience along predetermined pathways for the sake of achieving certain empirical results. In other words, the difficulty is not with the particular diagnostic measures we employ to assess learning; rather, it is with how we then use those measures.

# 10

# CONTINUUMS OF LEARNING

The single best way to motivate students to learn without the use of grades, tests, or test scores is to simply extend the continuums of learning for different subject matters more fully into the adult world and culture that young people inhabit. If students are able to see just how far subject areas in science, mathematics, language arts, social sciences, and the arts might extend into the world outside the classroom door and also into the culture and fabric of their own lives, then this more expanded viewpoint might well generate greater interest in their academic learning.

When young people are taught advanced knowledge that they do not usually associate with being in school within the context of traditional subject areas found in science or mathematics, or when they are taught subjects like history or art by extending these more fully into the world or culture in which they presently live, those areas of learning tend to become much more engaging.

That is, if students can directly perceive the actual scope of where lessons in different subject areas might eventually lead if they are extended into the larger adult world that is inherently so intriguing to many of them, then those subject areas will become more interesting. At the same time, those students will tend to be motivated to learn the basics of a particular area as they come to realize the reasons for acquiring those basics as precursors for learning about larger, more complex, and more intriguing fields of human endeavor.

One of the small group classes that was held at The Children's School was a class in human and childhood development in which the students, who were all between the ages of eleven and fourteen, studied different theories, from Freud to Jung to Rudolf Dreikurs to Jean Piaget. By far, the theory that had the biggest effect on the students was Piaget's theory of cognitive development.

Because the students were able to learn specifically how, according to Piaget, children and adolescents move, step by step, from concrete to representational to full abstract thought in conceptualizing their world, they were able to begin to look into the mirror of their own evolving cognitive development. Consequently, they actually began, in many cases, to observe many of their own thought processes and perceptions of their immediate social environment.

However, what became even more interesting was to watch many of these older students then begin to observe the behavior of the younger children in the classroom in light of what they were learning about cognitive development. In fact, in a number of different instances, these older students even developed a certain degree of compassion for younger students as they began to comprehend that they were operating on an entirely different cognitive level. Here was a very direct example of how certain academic learning that was expanded immediately into the larger social world that students inhabit could leave a real impression upon them.

Of course, we as educators can manipulate students to learn through the use of grades and tests. Or we can coerce them into learning certain knowledge and information by threatening them with being personally exiled in some manner from the acceptance of the larger school community. And we can even condition many of them into accepting these forms of approval as positive entities that they will want to embrace as a means of feeling better about themselves.

Yet there is something that we cannot do. We cannot fool young people into believing that they have a genuine interest in the content of a subject matter when that interest doesn't really exist. If young minds are not naturally attracted to the information and knowledge that is directly in front of them or to the manner in which that information and knowledge is presented, then educators can try to fool themselves by dealing with lack of interest through the sort of false gratification engendered in students by the different results-driven, manipulative devices that many schools presently employ.

Yet one cannot change a fact that is staring one in the face. That is, one cannot twist a young person's arm for the purpose of creating an interest in something that doesn't really exist. However, one can extend the continuums of learning in different subject areas so that what young people might learn in a particular area tends to become more interesting to them so that they are more easily engaged by it.

Yes, students need to learn subject matter in a sequential manner that permits them to assimilate certain skills and information before other skills and information will make sense to them. However, there is definitely a way to teach young people from the top down, so to speak, so that they can learn more basic knowledge by incorporating it into broader, more advanced areas of learning with which they have already had some experience. This has to do primarily with instructing students in exactly how the more advanced subject matter is constructed from the more basic pieces of knowledge, much as a jigsaw puzzle is constructed from its separate pieces.

## CHAPTER 10

If one can first see the puzzle as an organic whole, it then makes it much easier to see how the separate parts of it fit together. In the same fashion, if students can see just how the latest developments in a certain area of science were achieved primarily by correctly fitting together more basic knowledge and information, then those more basic aspects of the subject area tend to become more meaningful.

If students can begin to comprehend how certain contemporary cultural, political, or social events that inherently interest them are very much a function of how particular historical events have come together to produce them, then those historical events are less likely to become stagnant, inert events from the past. Instead, they will tend to become much more a part of current, living realities.

If young people can be assisted in visualizing the more practical, real-world uses for basic skills such as mathematics or writing, then the development of those skills may well come to feel to them much less like "schoolwork" that is exclusively part of an adult agenda. Instead, developing these skills might actually come to feel like something that the students are purposely giving themselves so that they can then tie the skills to more practical, real-world applications that are naturally more interesting.

A number of examples of this sort of "real-world" education took place at The Children's School. One was the weekly writers' conferences at which students journeyed together to one of the local coffee houses to read their pieces of writing to each other over hot chocolate or coffee, and during which they received constructive criticism from their fellow writers. If this had taken place inside the schoolhouse door, it would have felt simply like writing class at The Children's School. However, the fact that it took place in a local coffee house, reminiscent of certain beat poets from the fifties reading their poetry to each other, often brought the skill of learning to write much more into the social world outside the schoolhouse door.

Another example of this more real-world education was the weekly architectural drawing class, during which a small group of interested students journeyed each week to some famous Chicago landmark—Wrigley Field, the Baha'i Temple, the very modern State of Illinois Building downtown—and sharpened their drawing skills by attempting to individually draw these examples of unique architecture. Again, if we had simply had drawing class back at school, there would not have been the same immediate connection to the world outside the schoolhouse door.

Experts in learning have long known that if what one learns—particularly what young people in their formative years learn—cannot be fitted into the context of something much larger and more meaningful, it not only becomes less interesting but it is also assimilated less easily. Consequently, it tends not to remain with the learner for any significant period of time, and yet we consistently violate this cardinal rule about learning over and over again in our schools.

By continually segmenting subject areas into tightly defined units on which students will be eventually tested, and in which there is often so little connection between a particular subject area and what occurs in the world outside of school, we cause young people to have little or no idea why the subject might be of genuine interest to them.

Of course, once again, logical, sequential learning is absolutely necessary for young people. No educator worth his or her salt would ever argue with that. However, it is still possible to teach students by showing them how the advanced endpoints of a certain area of knowledge are composed of more basic ideas, skills, information, historical developments, and practical considerations that inexorably gravitate toward these endpoints. Then, when one goes back to teach this more basic knowledge, young people may be more interested in learning it simply because they can directly see where it eventually leads.

CHAPTER 10

Particularly because young people's impressions are so sharp and clear and also because they are actually in the process of forming opinions of what school and learning mean to them, this is the best time to give them an expanded view of different subject matters. If they can become more aware at an early age of just how the skills they are learning and the knowledge they are acquiring are part of an extended world of complex, interesting, real-life concerns, both learning and school might become more interesting to them.

As a result, they might also become more motivated to develop unique approaches of their own toward various knowledge and subject matters. Then, as their interests become piqued in this manner, this expanded view of education and learning may indeed remain as they grow older.

Unfortunately, what often works against this more expansive approach toward learning transpiring in our schools is the whole overorganized, limiting nature of the structure of most schools themselves. By carefully segmenting students' learning into tightly controlled units upon which they will be tested and evaluated empirically, we often end up keeping young people an arm's length away from the entire spectrum of learning with which they might become involved in various subject areas.

However, if teachers are going to be able to better assist students in how to create learning progressions from interests of theirs that are genuine so that both learning and school might become more interesting, then those teachers need to be allowed by schools to explore subject matters with their students that lie further along various continuums. Teachers need to be given more latitude than they are presently given in acquainting their students more fully with the advanced, more relevant, more real-world material that can then be tied to basic subject matter.

Unfortunately, today's teachers are often required to focus so exclusively on the basic material that prepares students for certain high-stakes evaluations of their learning that this more expanded approach to learning tends to be ruled out from its inception.

However, once again, if young people can become more familiar with a certain subject area—whether it be science, history, mathematics, writing, art, or geography—by being assisted in both visualizing and conceptually comprehending the more advanced places toward which the particular subject area is eventually headed, then they will be able to more easily assimilate the basic information and skills from that area. As a result, the more basic material will tend to be more interesting to them when they are better able to see exactly how it is related to the more advanced areas and knowledge of which it is a part.

At the same time, attempting to motivate young people to learn certain basic material that is not naturally interesting to them by rewarding them with grades, or through the use of other manipulative devices, is inherently deceitful because it means casting material and knowledge that students might comprehend as boring in an interesting light. As a consequence, young people begin to doubt their capacity to determine for themselves what might be of genuine interest to them.

Teachers can also assist young people in developing a much clearer point of view toward different subject matters by actually showing them extended continuums for different subject matter in advance so that the learning becomes more interesting. Of course, for teachers instructing their students in areas such as biological and physical sciences or the arts, in which the endpoints for a particular continuum are either extremely advanced or else constantly changing, this is admittedly not easy to do.

However, even though this would involve classroom teachers familiarizing themselves more fully with the latest developments in various fields of human endeavor so that they can present learning continuums to their students that give them the most

# CHAPTER 10

expansive view possible on what they are studying, it seems that this would be well worth the effort in terms of increased student interest.

For example, the group of students at The Children's School who were building a small strand of the DNA molecule from gumdrops and toothpicks while using an organic chemistry text had occasion to discuss with each other, and with myself, how genetic research might one day be able to actually change the structure of someone's DNA in order to prevent certain illnesses and medical conditions. Consequently, some of these students had now given themselves a much broader context into which they might place the subjects of human biology and genetics in terms of how they might potentially affect their own health and well-being as they grow older.

Likewise, another group of students, prior to some of them studying either basic geometry or architectural drawing, constructed different examples of cutting-edge modern architecture from photographs in books and Lego blocks. When they later came to learn geometry or made their own architectural drawings, some of them did so with an expanded idea of the inherent relationship between the study of geometry and that of architecture.

Similarly, a group of students who are learning about the history of the American Civil War might begin by learning, at a level they can understand, about certain aspects of contemporary African American culture or race relations in this country that genuinely interest them. Then, after enough time has been devoted to these, their teacher could go back with them to the causes of the Civil War, and relate their understanding of contemporary black culture and race relations to the origin of the conflict in 1860 so that the students might begin to comprehend exactly where it has led over time.

## CONTINUUMS OF LEARNING

In addition, while extending the scope of learning for a group of students for a specific subject area, teachers might be well advised to keep in mind that, once they have exposed those young people to a more expanded continuum for that area, it then becomes possible to move back and forth along that particular continuum in learning both more advanced and also more basic material. In other words, because the students have already become acquainted with the more complex material that lies further down the road, so to speak, their point of view in learning how the more basic material eventually leads toward the more advanced can be continually sharpened.

In terms of this, the Internet and World Wide Web are now highly significant allies. Because both students and their teachers can now have immediate access to advanced knowledge and information in any number of different subject areas, classroom teachers no longer have to depend so fully on their own expertise in extending continuums of learning for their students. Therefore, educators now have the opportunity to exponentially expand the scope of different subject areas. Consequently, they are now in a much better position to work with their students to develop learning progressions of their own, based on their interests, for two different reasons.

One, of course, is simply that, with instant access to information and knowledge from those who are genuine experts in particular fields of endeavor, students can now use that increased access to approach a particular subject matter from any number of different directions. That is, because their point of view for different learning areas can now be so greatly expanded through the immediate retrieval of expert information and knowledge in those areas, they now have many more opportunities to develop workable learning progressions of their own that stem from those expanded viewpoints.

## CHAPTER 10

Whether it's accessing the exponentially increasing number of websites that offer cutting-edge information to young people in any number of different areas or e-mailing university professors or experts from the world of work who are willing to communicate with students, there is a great opportunity here.

Advanced knowledge is often immediately available to students, so their teachers can now work with them to imagine, in greatly expanded fashion, the almost limitless number of places toward which learning in a particular subject area might gravitate. Hence, they now have a much greater opportunity to develop unique, workable learning progressions of their own simply because the fields of knowledge to which they now have access have become so greatly expanded.

This leads to the second reason: Because students can now access so much information on their own through the World Wide Web rather than depend on their classroom teacher to provide it for them, their teachers now have potentially more time to work with them to develop both a significant point of view toward a particular subject area and unique, interesting, workable learning progressions of their own in accessing that area. Consequently, that increased time and energy might now be put into assisting students in thinking more creatively about how they might want to approach various subject matters in a way that genuinely intrigues them.

Much of what students formerly had to either commit to memory or else research extensively in either the school or local library is now immediately available to them on the Web. And even though a certain sorting-out process is going to have to take place between information and knowledge that one needs to acquire for oneself and that which can simply be retrieved, young people are now able to simply retrieve so much of what before they needed to spend an extensive amount of time and energy learning.

As a result, there is now the possibility for a significant amount of time being made available to classroom teachers that formerly wasn't available to them. Consequently, there is now the opportunity to not only bring in all sorts of advanced, real-world subject matter that one traditionally doesn't associate with being in school but also work with students in accessing this material.

However, if this is going to occur, it is imperative that classroom teachers are not required to spend the inordinate amount of time that they now do either implementing predetermined curricula aimed primarily at achieving certain empirical test results or else simply preparing students for the tests themselves. These two things presently require so much time and energy on the part of teachers that to add to that this more expanded approach in which teachers are now researching and then introducing their students to ever more advanced subject matter would obviously soon become overwhelming.

Surely, if one is able to look at the purposes of education with an expanded, clear perspective, it should be obvious that facilitating student interest so that what young people are learning becomes increasingly meaningful to them should trump results-driven, empirical evaluations of learning nearly every time. However, by limiting subject matter for students to that on which they will be eventually tested—which is increasingly becoming the case—instead of expanding continuums of learning so that increased student interest might more closely bind their learning to their personal experience while they learn in an increasingly creative fashion, we are so often today standing the purpose of education on its head in a thoroughly negative manner.

# ABOUT THE AUTHOR

**Lyn Lesch** has been a classroom teacher for twenty-four years. After teaching in other schools for twelve years, he founded and directed The Children's School of Evanston, Illinois, a school for students ages six to fourteen, for another twelve years. The school received significant recognition from all of the major Chicago print and electronic media as a unique, innovative concept in education.

www.ingramcontent.com/pod-product-compliance
Lightning Source LLC
Chambersburg PA
CBHW021851300426
44115CB00005B/117